Potsdamer Platz
A History in Words and Pictures

Potsdamer Platz
A History in Words and Pictures

With contributions by
Ulrike Plewnia, Horst Mauter, László F. Földényi,
Ulrich Pfeiffer, Alfred Kernd'l and Thies Schröder

Translated by
Michael Robinson

NiSHEN

List of Illustrations

© 1996, 1st english edition
Verlag Dirk Nishen GmbH & Co. KG,
Bülowstrasse 66, 10783 Berlin
© 1991, © 1996 in the texts with the authors
© 1991, © 1996 in the illustrations with the photographers and lenders
Printed in Germany. All rights reserved.
Reproductions of any kind are forbidden.
Printing and binding: Bosch-Druck, Landshut

Verlag Dirk Nishen thanks all those involved and readers for their helpful hints.

ISBN 3 88940 334 4

Contents

Ulrike Plewnia

Exit the Myth, Enter the Patrons

Unduly solemn classical music does not easily put party-guests in the right mood, especially on building sites. And digging the first turf and topping-out ceremonies are celebrated with wild parties in Berlin. A sense of new beginnings after decades of dreariness. The boom is being celebrated. Clients commissioning new buildings are no longer content with champagne and canapés on these occasions. They go all out for culture, even on Europe's largest inner-city building site in Potsdamer Platz. Investors like Daimler-Benz subsidiary debis, Sony, A + T (ABB/Terreno-Roland Ernst), Hertie, the Senate as well as the Deutsche Bahn AG discovered this place at the point where east meets west, deserted until the Wall fell, and saw it as a potential showplace for self-representation. They are using this gigantic stage amidst cranes and bulldozers for architainment. They present themselves and their projects with increasingly unusual spectacles involving dancing, singing, music and performance, thus making them familiar long before completion.

The Berlin building boom has created a new field of activity for musicians and many other artists. Fear of excessive provision meant that the initial euphoria in the property market has long been somewhat dampened. For this reason marketing strategies are attempting to place investment premises that may have been costed too high as "classy addresses" well before the actual letting phase. Many project developers and building speculators may well have altruistic motives for their cultural commitment as well, but the identity and image factor – these are the current buzzwords – that is so crucial in marketing is the real reason for their cultural enthusiasm. In any case, the Berlin art scene is certainly benefiting from sudden commitment from patrons in its constant wrestling for subsidies.

Sony, the electronics firm, also laid on cultural festivities to celebrate when building started on its European headquarters and Sony Center designed by star architect Helmut Jahn. The "Oriol" chamber orchestra had difficulty in making its presence felt against the loud party atmosphere created by the first-turf-cutting smart set on the building site. But at least one important guest was impressed. Board chairman Norio Ohga, himself a trained musician and conductor, smilingly filmed the classical ensemble's specially composed wind fanfare. Proximity to the Philharmonie had been not the least of Ohga's reasons for choosing the site.

II

Daimler-Benz subsidiary debis also set standards from the beginning; they are in a position to boast about the most exquisite architecture in Potsdamer Platz. They sponsored avant-garde performances by the fringe theatre "Zum Westlichen Stadthirschen" in Weinhaus Huth, which along with the Grand Hotel Esplanade is the last reminiscence of times past. It also promoted the growing city within a city with a traditional "building site summer" of pop and jazz concerts in a tent. In summer 1995 debis surprised us with a première in a hitherto unknown dimension directly on the building site.

The "Pyro Space Ballet" danced in the shell of star Japanese architect Arata Isozaki's building to spectacular lighting effects and laser comic strips, cascades of fire and water sculptures. Spectators at the multicultural show "Beyond the Night" were treated to heavenly Vivaldi melodies, African bongo rhythms and hard techno-beat all performed on the floor slab, which had only just been concreted. Even the capital's arts critics, in the middle of their summer rest, took notice of this spectacle and enthused about the magnificent settings in this unusual place – actually a contemptible building site. The Swabian firm made the computer-controlled total artwork its present to the people of Berlin, plagued as they are with building work.

The concerns also present the arrival and launch of a giant dredger on a ground-water lake or the grotesque looking move of parts of the former Grand Hotel Esplanade as events for our spiritual edification. But the investors' most convincing coup in terms of self-representation, and the most important for the public, has been the building of the futuristic INFO BOX next door in Leipziger Platz. It was opened in October 1995 and since then this space-ship-like temporary structure has been

Building site summer for Daimler-Benz subsidiary debis, 1995 (see also page I left)

29 October 1994: laying the foundation stone for the Daimler-Benz project in Potsdamer Platz

attracting outsiders and Berliners almost like a magnet. The investors are exhibiting their metropolitan dreams and building visions on three storeys. They inform and entertain vividly with every conceivable contemporary medium, using drawings, models, films, animations and computers. Myths of the past are omitted. It is only about here, now and tomorrow. And now the masses are coming and reconquering Potsdamer Platz for themselves.

Roland Ernst, the jovial Heidelberg large-scale project developer, has also put his finger on it: "You can't reach people with boring advertisements any more today." But he certainly needs some ideas for cultural revaluation of the faceless monumental architecture he has thought up with ABB. The cool presentation in the A + T cabinet in the INFO BOX with austere drawings of façades and busts of architects does not make Grassi, Sawade and Co.'s punctuated grid monotony any more appealing.

But the project should suit conservative architecture critic Vittorio Lampugnani. For him addiction to self-representation in the building trade goes hand in hand with increasing "individualization of architecture". He too feels that the slack period means that the investors need prime addresses more than ever. Lampugnani: "This is why they get involved in a race for the most striking buildings, the most spectacular forms." For him, combining commerce and art on the building site is

8 September 1995: digging the first turf for the Sony Center am Potsdamer Platz

only a further excrescence of this trend that is so threatening to healthy urban development.

However, the pressurized developers' pompous search for a high profile does inspire other creative talents. Thus Matten Vogel, a graduate of the Hochschule der Künste, amuses himself by caricaturing the frenzied building in the sometime wilderness that was Potsdamer Platz – this son of an architect put up a building sign he had designed in the Ministergärten, site of the future Land delegacies: "Here Matten Vogel is building 1 detached house." This work of art was very soon stolen.

Building site summer for debis, 1994

V

Berlin's central area has a short but striking history. The urban development situation, focused on Potsdamer Platz, means that architectural, planning and transport schemes will appear here in the next few years. The intention is to link up with the historic place that has been destroyed and design a square that is new and open to the world; this makes the central area, and above all Potsdamer Platz, a part of Berlin that will see many developments.

The "first building" on the site, the INFO BOX, has been providing information on Europe's largest building site since October 1995. The exhibitions create a comprehensible vision of Berlin in the year 2000.

The building is based on designs by architects Schneider + Schumacher, Frankfurt am Main. Exhibitions are being mounted by: A + T, baulog, Bewag, Daimler-Benz, Deutsche Bahn AG, Deutsche Telekom AG, the Senate Building, Housing and Transport Department, Sony/Tishman Speyer/Kajima and the Magnetschnellbahn Planungsgesellschaft mbH (MPG).

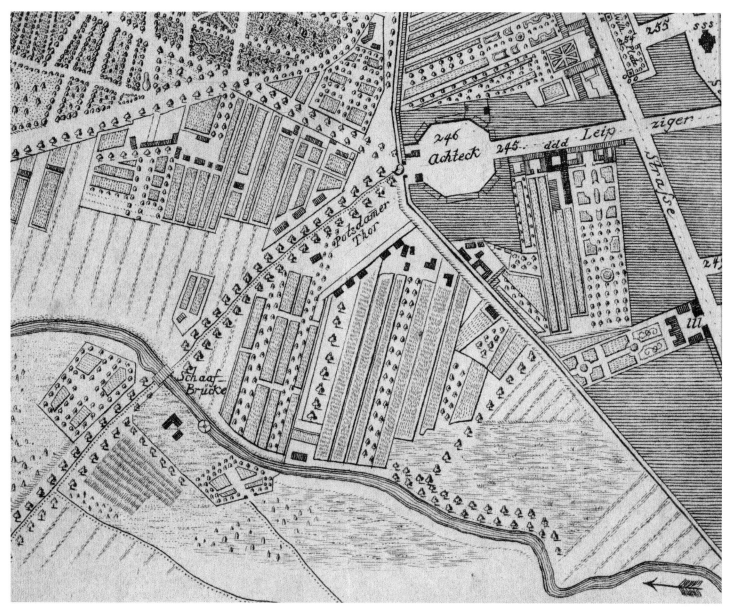

Ground plan of the royal Residence in Berlin
Carl Ludwig von Oesfeld, 1778

The excise wall, completed in 1737, also borders the town by the Potsdamer Tor behind the "Octogon". The area in front of it is used largely for farming and gardening. Summerhouses like individual buildings in gardens have sprung up on what were later to be Tiergarten-, Bellevue- and Hirschelstrasse and in Potsdamer Strasse. What was later to be Potsdamer Platz is recognizable only as a point where five streets or paths debouch by the gate.

Horst Mauter

Potsdamer Platz in Changing Times

It is said that squares, avenues, streets and alleyways in a city can be compared with the folds and wrinkles in a person's face. Just like these they give the city its atmosphere, a quite particular expression, its unmistakable personal qualities. They change continually, and shape the city's character; they make it impinge upon our consciousness as beautiful and remarkable, or make us forget it rapidly as nondescript.

It is striking that we identify cities particularly strongly with their squares, we recognize them as soon as their names are mentioned: Place de la Concorde, Forum Romanum, Wenceslas Square, Stachus, Red Square, Tiananmen Square – do we still need to mention the name of the city?

Potsdamer Platz is missing from this list. There is a special story behind this square, once one of the best known in Berlin, and now the subject of this book. History has played some dirty tricks on it. So dirty that many older people have almost forgotten it, and many of the younger ones do not even know where it used to be. All the squares mentioned above have their fates, and it would be interesting to write about them; many of them had their own catastrophes but they all remained squares that were part of their cities. But German history drove Potsdamer Platz into a kind of coma in the last few decades.

Potsdamer Platz became part of Berlin's existence after half a millennium of history. After a hundred years its development, hesitant at first, started to leap forward: it was soon on everybody's lips, for within a few decades it had blossomed from a square on the periphery of the royal residence into one of Berlin's central squares, in a city that had so suddenly become cosmopolitan. Its range of functions and pulsating life impressed its chroniclers to such an extent that they dramatically proclaimed it to be the "busiest square in Europe" (1935). Politicians, artists, globetrotters from all over the place and of course the Berliners themselves enthused about it: the square had grown so wildly, so far beyond itself and in such a short time, without the planning accuracy of architects and town planners, unlike its neighbour, Leipziger Platz, with which it later merged.

And then it seemed that this world-famous square was going to have to take all the blame for the mistaken policies of the Nazi German state, which had plunged the world into the most terrible of all wars: in a few nights of air-raids and a few days of fighting it sank into an immense sea of ruins that

The Schafbrücke outside the
Potsdamer Tor. On the right
are trees in Potsdamer Strasse
dating from the time of
Friedrich II.

Christian Gottfried Mathes,
etching, 1775

8

shattered the survivors. Potsdamer Platz was not to be resurrected from the ruins, it was razed to the ground, robbed of its outline, made part of the featureless waste of that border, many hundreds of kilometres long, that divided two worlds, "East and West", "Capitalism and Socialism", "Good and Evil" – or "Evil and Good"? – from each other. Was this the end of a square that used to be on the lips of every Berlin enthusiast? For almost thirty years it seemed it was.

But history took its course; the five metre high concrete wall that divided our square, the barrier between two worlds, for many people between life and death, was suddenly no more, without meaning and without purpose, after the people who were shut in had started to move, after the "unbloody revolution" of 1989. Day and night thousands of "Wall woodpeckers" were hammering souvenirs out of this monument with mallet and chisel, on the former site of Potsdamer Platz as well, and anything that looked decent was sold as a souvenir by the ton, all over the world.

Politicians in the East and in the West, architects and town planners, Berliners and many others are agreed: Potsdamer Platz, rich in tradition, need not have died for ever. It will be tracked down in the desert of the unassuming no-man's-land of history. It will rise again like a phoenix from the ashes and remind us of its interesting past. Then it will be what it was before its tragic decline: a synthesis of old and new, a link between the parts of a great and vibrant city, again on the lips of people from Berlin, from Germany and the whole world.

No Distinguishing Features

The Thirty Years War (1618 to 1648) left the Elector's residence of Berlin/Cölln and the other cities and villages of the electoral Mark Brandenburg in a sorry state. Several decades of energetic rebuilding were necessary to get over the consequences of war. It was not until 1680 that a phase of gradual upturn began that was probably first and most clearly visible in the development of Berlin and Cölln, the residence towns of Friedrich Wilhelm (1640–1688), Elector of Brandenburg and Prussia.

Since 1658 an immense effort had been made to transform them and Friedrichswerder into a fortress on the Dutch model. But soon there was not enough room between the ramparts and ditches for the many people who were moving in. From 1674, even before building work on the fortress had ended, the Dorotheenstadt was growing up to the west of it. After the mass immigration by Huguenot religious refugees after 1685 another town started to spring up west of the fortress from 1688 and this was named Friedrichstadt after the new Elector, who had followed his late father as ruler.

The first cartographic record of Berlin and its surroundings by an engineer called N. la Vigne dates from 1685. It recalls for us the situation of the site south of the Tiergarten, where Potsdamer Platz was later to grow up. The main axis of this area is the unfortified, sandy road that led over the Schafbrücke, mentioned even in the Middle Ages, and formed a link with the village of Schöneberg. It was later to become Potsdamer Strasse. The Elector chose this as his preferred route to Potsdam, where he had commissioned a prestigious development of the palace in 1660, which had fallen into disrepair, from Johann Gregor Memhard, who was to follow the Dutch model.

Potsdamer Strasse also had a branch leading to Leipzig, and so it became a long-distance link that was as important economically as it was politically. A "mail-coach to Leipzig" following this route was mentioned as early as 1690, and a dozen years later the "mounted mail", the "travelling mail" and the "mail-coach" provided a service between the two cities several times a day – provided they were not preventing from passing the Schafgraben (later Landwehrkanal) waterway by major flooding in spring. La Vigne's map shows us that the Schafgraben, cut from Potsdamer Strasse, was flanked by large meadows on either side. It must have taken its name from their use as pasture for sheep.

An important area that was later to increase the significance of Potsdamer Platz saw far-reaching changes in this decade. A good way north-east of the old Schafbrücke (bridge) a route running north-west branched off from the Potsdamer Landstrasse. It led to the Elector's Tiergarten (game reserve), which dated from the 15th century and occupied the whole of the area between Berlin/Cölln and the village of Lietzow (also Lützow, later Charlottenburg), whose southern fences ran along the Schafgraben meadow. Elector Friedrich Wilhelm had a sturdy fence built around the area, which had become overgrown, and all the animals had disappeared during the Great War. The Tiergarten was restocked with game from many places, so that after a time it became a well-maintained hunting area once more.

The whole area had acquired greater significance ever since Electress Charlotte had commissioned the first work on the magnificent place of Charlottenburg that was named in her honour after her death as the first queen of Prussia in 1705. A new development phase in the Tiergarten aimed to drain it and open up routes through it. Communications between Berlin and the new palace at Lietzow were greatly improved. First attempts to make the Tiergarten prestigious and park-like also date from this time. And so the Elector's hunting ground, the game reserve that had been so carefully built up again, went through its first metamorphosis – into a royal pleasure-ground for the whole colourful and elegant crowd of courtiers and other nobility.

Even then the Tiergarten had several southern access points from the path that ran along it on the Schafgraben meadow side (later Tiergartenstrasse). The more the Tiergarten moved into the public eye the more frequently these were used for getting into and out of it. It was at this early date that the first settlement activities started in the immediate vicinity of the site on which Potsdamer Platz was later to come into being. Several émigré French gardeners settled on the peripheral route and created blossoming gardens and cultivated fields from the green meadows and areas of sand. In the mean time it was not just the Berlin nobility who sought out their green surroundings in the finer seasons or strolled through the restful Tiergarten on Sundays and holidays, it had become the done thing for the bourgeoisie as well. The French colonists welcomed any additional source of income, and so they let summer accommodation in their houses and provided tenants and strollers with coffee, other drinks and simple food.

Das Leipziger Thor. *La porte de Leipsic.*

The old Potsdamer Tor with military guard-house (right) and customs post (left). By the right-hand pier of the gate the excise wall, completed in 1737, can be made out. It was intended to help to prevent customs avoidance and desertion by soldiers. It divided Leipziger Platz from Potsdamer Platz. Friedrich August Calau, aquatint, c. 1820

11

From Modest Beginnings

In the early 18th century the feudalist-absolute system of government took a complete hold as the Prussian state coalesced. This also increased the significance of the residence on the Spree. Important events were drawing international attention to Germany at the time. Friedrich III's great rival August the Strong (1694–1733) had added the title of King of Poland to that of Elector of Saxony by personal union (1697), and so the Prussian Elector was looking for a rise in rank. After protracted negotiations with the German Emperor he placed the crown on his own head a long way from Berlin in the Prussian town of Königsberg on 18 January 1701, and could now call himself King of Prussia.

The King tried to demonstrate his enhanced status sumptuously to Berlin and the world with lavish and expensive court life. The residence towns of Berlin, Cölln, Friedrichswerder, Dorotheenstadt and Friedrichstadt, along with some suburbs, were brought together in 1709/10 as the united residence of Berlin. The Prussian kings preferred it to the other towns in the state in every respect, in terms of urban development and architecture as well. Thus it developed into the administrative, economic and cultural centre of feudal-absolutist state life and grew from decade to decade.

Friedrich Wilhelm I (1713–1740), known as the "Soldier King", made the city into the state's largest garrison. But he also stabilized the economic base and continued to plan and execute extensions to the residence. In 1732 the last 400 Friedrichstadt parcels were built on to Mauerstrasse, and by then the extensions to the south and west that had been planned as early as 1723 were completed under the direction of Colonel Christian Reinhold von Derschau (1679–1742) and architect Philipp Gerlach the Younger (1679–1748). A geometrical grid of streets had been created in the first Friedrichstadt building phase, following typical baroque urban development ideas. This was concluded with a generous frame whose main axis was formed by Wilhelmstrasse, with deep gardens on the western side. A special feature of the baroque development was the establishment of three large squares on the urban periphery, each at the end of a main street. And so the "Quarree" (later Pariser Platz) was built in the north at the end of Unter den Linden, in the south the "Rondell" (now Mehringplatz), below the junction of Friedrich-, Linden- and Wilhelmstrasse, and in the centre the "Octogon" (later Leipziger Platz) at the end of Leipziger Strasse. The squares were intended as mustering and parade grounds for soldiers billeted in the bourgeois houses, and also drew off some marketing activity from the inner city. This latter plan did not work out for the Octogon.

The developments in Wilhelmstrasse are of interest to us. In the southern section terrace-like, two-storey building with modest but pleasing façades were felt to be adequate. But north of Kochstrasse a series of palaces for the nobility grew up from 1734 to 1736. These were architectural masterpieces of their period. The majority of them remained as examples of mature baroque architecture until they were destroyed in the Second World War. The designs were by some of the best early 18th century architects, for example Jean de Bodt (1670–1745), Friedrich Wilhelm Dieterichs (1702–1782), Konrad Wiesend as well as Philipp Gerlach the Younger (1679–1748). The palaces built for Baron von Vernezobre and Graf von der Schulenburg, the count's Beeßische Palace for Privy Councillor Kellner, the palace of Herzog Friedrich von Braunschweig, the palaces of Graf von

Schwerin and of President von Görne, the palaces for the counts of Finckenstein and for the Master of the Order of St. John of Jerusalem were particularly remarkable.

Two-storey, harmoniously urban buildings, some quite densely developed, but others designed more in the palace style, were also built at the end of Leipziger Strasse and in the "Octogon". This accumulation of palaces for the nobility gave this part of the city a feel of feudal elegance even in its early days. The owners of these palaces were not just used to blustering at court, but in the main were directly involved in government business as state officials or generals.

The development of the extended Friedrichstadt with almost 1,000 dwellings was largely complete in a mere four years, as the King supported it lavishly with money and materials. But in the same way as he gave preferential treatment to all those noblemen and bourgeois who were prepared to build here at their own expense, he also used his administrative power rigorously in order to achieve his ends. The city's craft guilds were compelled to set up workshops in Friedrichstadt, even if they thought that new ones were not really necessary. Baron Vernezobre was able to prevent his daughter from being married as the King desired only by building his magnificent palace in Wilhelmstrasse at his own expense. And so guilds and private individuals were often thrust into considerable debt and some even brought to the brink of financial ruin.

Subsequently to the development of Friedrichstadt the whole town, which has grown so much in the last few years, was surrounded by a palisade or wall over eight kilometres long, passable through thirteen gates. This wall and gate system was partly intended to prevent customs fraud. It was also intended to make it more difficult for soldiers in the Berlin garrison to desert, a problem that was assuming mass proportions. And so all these gates had an excise collection point and a constant military guard.

The "Octogon", set at the exit from the city on busy Leipziger or Potsdamer Strasse, acquired one of these gates in 1735 – the Potsdamer Tor. It stood out among the other pier buildings because of its detailed architectural design and lavish decoration – as did the Brandenburger Tor in its early version. Contemporary plans show clearly that there was an excise- and a guard-house behind the pier building in Potsdamer Platz as well.

Friedrichstadt had now thrust forward to the line at which Potsdamer Platz was starting to emerge beyond the gate. The "Octogon" had been sensibly projected on the drawing-board by the architects as a main square within the baroque ensemble. However, the square outside the gate developed without planning, to meet certain functional requirements, as it were from a "rank root".

Essentially this new square grew from the fact that several streets or paths led to Potsdamer Platz from various directions. The most important of them was still the one that led to Potsdam, where the amount of traffic was constantly increasing. It also dominated as a traffic artery for Saxony. The city's rapid development under the Soldier King – in 1713 there were 220 buildings, but already 1152 by 1740 – was not simply for military reasons. The commercial upturn brought increasing travel with it, and so did the fact that Friedrich II (1740–1786) in particular ruled his state from Potsdam for long periods, which increased the latter's political and cultural importance. Barouches belonging to

Berlin panorama. The wooden palisade built after the first Friedrichstadt development phase up to 1720 runs along Mauerstrasse. On the left at the edge of the picture Unter den Linden, the street leading to the centre, can be seen. Leipziger Strasse runs this side of the fortifying moat on the right by the old Leipziger Tor (14).

Friedrich Bernhard Werner, copperplate engraving, c. 1720

courtiers, various noblemen, high officials and officers were soon taken for granted by the inhabitants of the villages that lay along these roads.

But the significance of Potsdamer Platz was also increased for local reasons. The most important of these was the more rapid development of Schöneberg. It had been resettled after devastation in the Thirty Years War, and under Friedrich II it was chosen as a starting point for occupation by twenty Bohemian weaving and spinning families, as part of the commercial settlement policy. The colonists had favourable conditions for establishing themselves north of Schöneberg on both sides of

Potsdamer Strasse on the "waste sandhill". This "independent village" was closely linked with to the Mühlenhof office in Berlin and its city council, and Berlin merchants organized work and the sale of goods. The Bohemians also retained close connections with their community in Friedrichstadt, sharing its parish and school. And so it is not surprising that Potsdamer Strasse was an important traffic artery for them.

The Botanical Gardens were beside the Bohemian settlement, on the Berlin side. These took their first major upturn in the reign of Friedrich II, who appointed Johann Gottlieb Gleditsch (1714–1786), who achieved outstanding success here, in the fields of forestry and agriculture. This jewel attracted interested botanists from many countries.

Even contemporaries realized the increasing importance of the road leading from the Potsdamer Tor to Potsdam. The Prussians were starting to improve their road system by laying made-up "Chausseen", and Potsdamer Strasse was the first to be "chausséed" from 1791 to 1793, under the direction of Carl Gotthard Langhans (1732–1808), who created the Brandenburger Tor. The bridge over the Schafgraben, the later Potsdamer Bridge, was also rebuilt as part of this work, but still as a wooden structure.

Another route that greatly influenced the emergence of Potsdamer Platz was the link between Potsdamer Tor and the Huguenots' estate on the southern edge of the Tiergarten. At the end of this, a farmstead dating from 1716 became the headquarters of the "Hofjäger" (court hunter), who was responsible for the Tiergarten land, even before 1750. After 1770 an innkeeper called Hahn set up an establishment here that rapidly became the most popular source of refreshment for trippers and walkers because of its romantic situation on the Schafgraben at the corner of the Tiergarten. It is said that the court came here rather than anywhere else. In any case the Tiergarten had become a park used for strolling and pleasure by an increasing number of Berliners. Hans Georg Wenzeslaus von Knobelsdorff (1699–1753) had been regularly at work on improving it since 1742, creating star patterns and avenues running all over the park. In several places he had it redesigned in the French style, with inscrutable labyrinths and attractively shaped pools. In this context the avenue from the Brandenburger Tor to Charlottenburg was straightened and made up.

The route from Potsdamer Platz to the path on the southern periphery of the Tiergarten now met this avenue, making it the most important road link between Charlottenburg and south Berlin via the Potsdamer Tor. Knobelsdorff has set up a dairy and had a country house built for himself in the northern part of the park, directly on the Spree, in 1743. This changed hands several times after his death, until Friedrich II's youngest brother, Prince August Ferdinand (1730–1813), had Schloß Bellevue built on this site by Philipp Daniel Boumann the Younger (1747–1803) from 1785. It went into architectural history as the first royal Prussian palace to be unambiguously neo-classical. The road from Potsdamer Tor to Charlottenburger Allee was now taken through to Schloß Bellevue.

Further sandy but soon ever more frequently used routes outside and inside the length of the excise wall also started from Potsdamer Platz. In the north, in the direction of the Brandenburger Tor, they were called the Brandenburgische Communication, and in the south towards Hallesches Tor the Potsdamer Communication. Development of these routes changed the situation in front of the "Octogon" in relation to the Potsdamer Tor to the extent that several citizens started to live there. King Friedrich Wilhelm I had exchanged a large part of the land between the Potsdamer Tor and the Tiergarten with the church in Lietzow when he was rounding off his game reserve. Sections of it were leased by the founder of the Realschule (secondary school) in Kochstrasse, consistorial councillor Johann Julius Hecker (1707–1768), who set up a school garden with a mulberry plantation on this land in 1753. For this reason the Communication north of the Potsdamer Tor became known as Schulgartenstrasse. A cemetery for the parish of Trinity ("Dreifaltigkeit") church came into being here as well.

Parts of the site south of the Potsdamer Tor had been parcelled even before 1770, and several Berliners, again including members of the French colony, settled between the Potsdamer Communication and Potsdamer Strasse. A number of sites were used by gardeners for commercial purposes, and others as summer resorts by citizens of various professions and positions. One of the best-known inhabitants was undoubtedly the flautist and composer Johann Joachim Quantz (1679–1773), who had played a not insignificant role at the court of Friedrich II and was also a member of the bourgeois-intellectual "Monday Club".

The remaining meadows and areas of land in Potsdamer Strasse were also parcelled and leased to gardeners and farmers. It was only after the "Chaussierung" of 1791 to 1793 that long-term residents and summer visitors settled here on any scale. At the turn of the century settlement had reached the Schafbrücke and moved beyond the Schafgraben to Schöneberg village property.

But all in all the area of the emerging Potsdamer Platz was quite thinly settled around 1800. Peter Haas's very precise Tierpark plan (1754–1804) does not show even three dozen built-up plots in the whole area between "Hofjäger", Potsdamer Tor, the Tiergarten and the Schafgraben. The one- and two-storey little houses, like farmhouses, rural houses or sometimes even villas are set back from the streets in gardens that sometimes seem quite idyllic. They give the area a thoroughly suburban look. It was not used commercially at all, if you forget about two dozen gardeners and one or two farmers from Charlottenburg and Schöneberg.

Some manufactories were established in the course of the 18th century, but only further afield: in the north there was a Russian leather factory and a calico bleaching house behind the Tiergarten on the Spree, a stocking maker by the Schafgraben up by the Hofjäger establishment and a cloth bleaching house at Hallesches Tor. The commercial premises nearest to Potsdamer Platz were inside the excise wall. Ernst Gotzkowsky (1710–1775) took over the silk factory at 3 Leipziger Strasse in the former Groebensches Haus in 1750, and made it into a flourishing business. He also opened a porcelain factory in the neighbouring Dervillsches Haus in 1761, and this passed into the King's hands as part of the crisis measures after the Seven Years War. It quickly acquired an international reputation as the Royal Porcelain Manufactory because of the quality and beauty of its products. In 1780 this manufactory had over 500 employees.

Mention of the Seven Years War is a reminder that Potsdamer Platz was starting to attract international political attention even at that time, even though it was not yet completely formed. Friedrich II had started his reign successfully with the two Silesian Wars (1740–1742, 1744/45), but his aggressive and ruthless policy against foreign interests left war open as a logical consequence from 1756 to 1763. When the king was in Silesia with his main force in 1760, on 3 October a Russian, and shortly afterwards an Austro-Saxon corps succeeded in besieging the southern gates of the residence on the Spree, occupying Charlottenburg and involving the Prussian troops in day-long skirmishes. The enemy had set up their artillery on the heights of Rixdorf and Schöneberg, but also – as a contemporary map shows – beyond the Schafgraben, close by Potsdamer Strasse and south-west of the Tiergarten, and were firing at Friedrichstadt from there. The enemy had also entrenched themselves in the Botanical Gardens. The whole of old Schöneberg burned down in violent fighting for access to the city on 7 October, and buildings and plants in the Botanical Gardens were severely damaged. Two days later the Residence was occupied. But the Russian and Austro-Saxon intruders soon withdrew, having relieved the Berliners of substantial contributions.

Friedrich II's aggressive policies had brought the state to the verge of ruin. But ultimately it was precisely this war that made Prussia a major European power at its end. Berlin now helped to shape European history, and Potsdamer Platz, that was still taking shape, and – just like the Residence – had narrowly escaped destruction, moved up several ranks in the value-scale for international squares.

In the period after the war the area in front of the Potsdamer Tor increasingly became a centre of recreation and pleasure. Popular inns, cafés and restaurants developed from the Huguenot settlers' small coffee houses, attracting crowds of Berliners on fine days. The Leipzig author Karl Heinrich Krögen (c. 1750–1788) described them after a visit to Berlin in 1783 with a hint of irony, but by no means unaffectionately:

"These (coffee gardens) were by the Potsdamer Tor, and their fronts faced the Tiergarten. And they were visited frequently. There are a few people there, and spacious rooms where one can enjoy oneself. … They are just as popular in winter as in summer, and on Sunday in particular one sees a numerous company of both sexes assembled, beguiling the hour with coffee, wine and chocolate. The women sit there, despite the quantities of tobacco smoke, among all the men swap stories about the city and the world, talk about finery and new fashions, or if the fancy takes them allow themselves to be entertained by male persons, until evening nears, when one leaves this place

of pleasure and seeks out other similar ones in the town."

The oldest of these establishments was in Charlottenburger Allee. It dated from 1725, in the form of an inn called "Zum letzten Heller" ("The Last Penny"). This inn was extended by the Huguenot Richard, and was later on named "Kemper-Hof" (Kemperplatz) after his successor. From here on westwards to the "Hofjäger" was a series of large and small establishments of this kind running the whole way down the street, belonging to Michaelis, George, Taron, Teichmann, Bayer and others. The concerts and fireworks they arranged were considered a particular attraction.

The summer visitors who rented houses outside the Potsdamer Tor area annually often enough included well-known personalities, like Henriette Herz (1764–1847) for example, who was highly admired for her beauty, intellectual agility and charm by the authorities on art and science who attended bourgeois salons. Each summer she lived in a house at 18 Tiergartenstrasse. As she was often seen on lengthy walks in the Tiergarten with her close friend of many years standing the theologian and philosopher Daniel Schleiermacher (1768–1834), even her great popularity and command could not protect her from suspicion and from caricatures.

August Wilhelm Iffland (1759–1814), Director General of the "Königliches Nationaltheater" in Gendarmenmarkt, had set up a comfortable home a few houses further west in 1801. He liked to have stimulating parties for major literary and musical figures in his home. He received his most famous visitor several times in spring 1804: Friedrich von Schiller (1759–1805) stayed in Berlin from 1 to 17 May, in order to decide whether or not to move here. The famous poet, who was enthusiastically

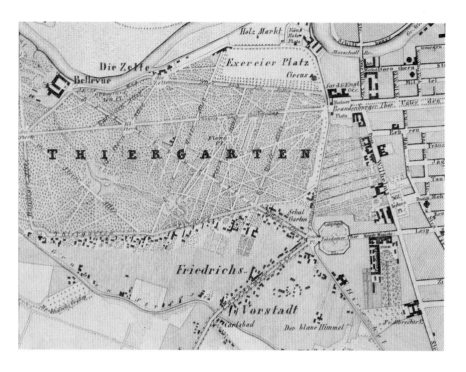

*Town plan of Berlin
Verlag der geographischen
Anstalt des Bibliotheks-
Institutes zu Hildburghausen,
1834 (detail)*

*Four years before the opening
of the Berlin-Potsdam Railway the out-of-town character
beyond Potsdamer Platz is
still clearly recognizable,
despite the increased number
of individual buildings. The
first buildings are appearing
immediately outside the gate,
the architectural completion
of the square is beginning.*

accepted in the Residence, met master mason and
founder of the Singing Academy Carl Friedrich
Zelter (1748–1832) in Iffland's house, and also
Johann Friedrich Unger (1753–1804), owner of the
Vossische Zeitung, and historian Karl Ludwig von
Woltmann (1770–1817), who were already friends
of long standing. His wife Lotte described Iffland's
house as an "ideal garden residence, whose bosky
hedge hid the sand in front of it".

A New Epoch

The relatively peaceful development of the
district by the Potsdamer Tor was again interrupted by significant international events in the
early 19th century, affecting the innermost parts of
Prussia. King Friedrich Wilhelm III's (1797–1840)
vacillating and indecisive policy in terms of alli-
ances had isolated Prussia internationally, so that it
became the plaything of Napoleon's expansionist
policy. This led to the battle of Jena and Auerstedt
on 14 October 1806, which ended in a catastrophic defeat for Prussia. A very few days later
French troops were advancing on Berlin. On 24
October the advance guard moved through Hallesches Tor into the Prussian Residence. Two days
later the people who lived around Potsdamer Platz
and Leipziger Strasse also experienced the spectacle
of entry by the colourful horde. At their head was
Marshall Louis Nicolas Davoust (1770–1832), no
stranger to victory. Representatives of the city
council rushed to hand him the keys of the city in
solemn fashion, thus offering command of the city;
but he sent the delegation and the keys to Potsdam,
and these were accepted by the emperor only when
he rode through the Brandenburger Tor on 27
October.

The national struggle for liberation from 1806 to
1815 did not end in a united German state. Prussia
was one of the victorious powers; to the regret of
its politicians it played only a second rank role in
international politics, but a by no means insignificant one. Berlin had asserted its position as the
political centre of this German state, the largest
after Austria. The reform movement that started in
1807 was very far-reaching. Agrarian reform, the
introduction of rigid trade regulations, financial
reform, changes to the customs system and early

stages in the emancipation of the Jews, and not least a through commercial promotion programme by the state were the main changes leading to full implementation of the industrial revolution, which also completely changed life in Berlin.

The Prussian capital increasingly became the economic centre of Prussia east of the Elbe. The textile industry remained the basis of economic life, in particular off-the-peg clothing, which expanded in leaps and bounds from the 1830s. Branches of capitalist industry also expanded, mechanical engineering and equipment construction, the chemical and cleaning industries, and the food, tea, coffee, alcohol industries. Berlin increasingly reinforced its role as a place for trade. The city became the most used stock-pile and shipment centre of the whole of Prussia east of the Elbe and beyond. An enormous variety of products from central Germany left its merchant's offices and warehouses for destinations all over the world.

And finally in the next decades Berlin became central Germany's banking metropolis. Around 1870 its Stock Exchange was already, after the Viennese and before those in Hamburg and Frankfurt, the most important in any German state. Bankers from almost all the Prussian provinces and from other German countries sought to be close to it, set themselves up in the Spree metropolis, founded branches or commissioned local bankers to represent them. "Berlin high finance" became a proverbial power in the state, with far-reaching influence on all spheres of its existence.

View through the Potsdamer Tor (gate), redesigned by Karl Friedrich Schinkel 1823/24. It was laid out to suit its old function: on the left is the military guard-house, on the right the customs house. The corner of Schulgarten- and Bellevuestrasse can be seen in the background.

Johann Heinrich Hintze/ William Barber, steel engraving, c. 1833

The expansion of Berlin was interrupted for a long time by the bellicose times of the Wars of Liberation. Then plans for change moved into the foreground, affecting Potsdamer Platz as well. Here a link was made with Carl Gotthard Langhans's successful redesign of the Brandenburger Tor in the period from 1788 to 1791. At the forefront of the discussion now was higher architectural status for the street, which was become increasingly busy, and the gate, which seemed particularly important in court circles. The great importance ascribed to this area is also expressed in the fact that in memory of the people's battle in Leipzig the "Octogon" had been renamed Leipziger Platz and the Potsdamer Tor had become the Leipziger Tor.

The rebuilding plans were realized by Karl Friedrich Schinkel in 1823/24. Appropriately to the gate's function as an excise collection point and military guardhouse he designed the complex in terms of two gatehouses flanking the street. They were given four-columned Gothic porticoes, reflecting the clear neo-classical attitudes of the time.

Peter Joseph Lenné (1789–1866) was commissioned to redesign Leipziger Platz. He successfully rounded off Schinkel's architectural achievement in a harmonious fashion. The two halves of the lawn were framed with iron fences of medium height in 1828 and planted only sparsely with trees and shrubs, thus stressing the austere peripheral development of the relatively spacious square with its baroque palaces and making it into a meaningful unit with the gateway.

Lenné had been working on plans for a thorough redesign of the Tiergarten since 1816, and he continued to modify them. He worked on the project for over one and a half decades, co-operating with Karl Friedrich Schinkel from time to time. His plans were realized from 1832. The design of the Tiergarten's south-eastern periphery had also been taken into consideration. The part of the "cannon route" leading from Schulgartenstrasse to Charlottenburger Allee was planned as a street with villas laid out like a park, and Lenné started to implement the plan himself. He had a villa-style house designed and built on the corner of Schulgartenstrasse by court building inspector Friedrich Ludwig Persius (1803–1845). He was given the plot and 7,000 talers towards the cost as a reward for his meritorious garden designs.

Overall the suburban character of this area between the Tiergarten and the Schafgraben with its markedly summer-residence and villa-style development had been reinforced, but nevertheless settlement here was being pushed ahead with considerable vigour. In the course of this development, between 1830 and 1840, the old, vernacular names of the paths had been replaced by names that did justice to a residential area of this kind. Potsdamer Platz, Potsdamer and Schulgartenstrasse retained their old names, Charlottenburger Allee was now called Bellevuestrasse, the street along the southern periphery of the Tiergarten Tiergartenstrasse, the cannon route Lennéstrasse and the Potsdamer Communication Hirschelstrasse.

The rapid economic upswing in the Prussian capital between 1815 and 1870 led to the development of preferred sites, to an ordering of commercial space, not absolute, but clearly recognizable. The mechanical engineering quarter outside the Oranienburger Tor, in Köpenicker Strasse up to Schlesisches Tor, the off-the-peg clothing area between the Werderscher Markt, Hausvogteiplatz and Leipziger Strasse, weaving in east and north-east Berlin, the concentration of over 300 banks (c. 1870) between show street Unter den Linden and Leipziger Strasse – these were focal points of commercial life in early capitalist times that anyone could recognize. The territory outside Potsdamer Tor also had its share in this development. Not that it had actually become a centre of government, industrial area or the seat of important banks or commercial enterprises. But as it was immediately adjacent to the city centre with all its accumulation of economic potential, set in an agreeably relaxing landscape, it became a popular residential area for the affluent: civil servants, officers, bankers, merchants and manufacturers. The 1836 Berlin directory already names 439 owner-occupier and tenant families (not including servants) in this area between the Tiergarten and the Landwehrkanal, between the Potsdamer Tor and what later became Regentenstrasse. The breakdown in terms of professions is interesting. The largest group was 88 families of low-grade civil servants, but there were also 59 of high-grade civil servants, 44 of businessmen, 29 of officers, 24 of bankers, brokers and with private incomes. Service-related occupations were strongly represented: 54 families of gardeners, 50 of craftsmen, 23 of architects, sculptors and painters, twelve of inn- and hotel-keepers, ten of musicians and singers. The remaining families were divided between various professional groups, each occurring fewer than ten times.

The extraordinarily high proportion of councillors of justice, legations, commerces and others and of privy councillors earned the district outside Potsdamer Platz – more soberly called "Friedrichvorstadt" – the title "Privy Councillors' Quarter", this was originally intended as a nickname, but was appropriate even at this early stage, as our socio-statistical analysis has shown.

View of the south-eastern corner of Leipziger Platz with Prince Adalbert of Prussia's palace. The end of Leipziger Strasse is on the right.

Carl Gaertner, water-coloured pen-and-ink drawing, 1842

SOMETHING OF A GATEWAY TO THE WORLD

The steam engine symbolized the rise of capitalism in the first half of the 19th century. It revolutionized not only the entire production process, but also transport. In its mobile form it also had a lasting effect on the fortunes of Potsdamer Platz. Working on English experience, and taking account of Friedrich List's forward-looking 1833 essay in which he postulated the significance of Berlin for a future German rail network, Berlin capitalists pressed for railway building based on Berlin with increasing vigour. Political, economic and military reasons meant that these plans were relatively quickly realized. The Berlin–Potsdam Railway Company organized the building of the line from Potsdam to Berlin. A partial service from Potsdam to Zehlendorf started first, and a good month later, on 29 October 1838, the whole line, over 26 km long, to the Potsdamer Bahnhof (station) outside the Potsdamer Tor was able to go into service. Ten years later the route was extended to Magdeburg, connecting Berlin with the west German and international networks.

Shortly after that, a mere 600 metres from the Potsdamer Bahnhof, another large station was built, the Anhalter Bahnhof. The service to Jüterbog started from here on 1 July 1841, and shortly afterwards to Dessau and Köthen. This established a connection with the Saxon railway network, and soon with southern Europe as well. The Anhalter Bahnhof was certainly more directly connected with Wilhelmstrasse, and thus with the centre, by Askanischer Platz and Anhaltische Strasse, but it soon became clear that Potsdamer and Leipziger Platz and Leipziger Strasse attracted visitors like a magnet. Thus the significance of Potsdamer Platz had increased enormously as a result of the intro-

The 18th and early 19th century garden houses have been almost completely forced out by multi-storey residential blocks. The "Eisbock", a garden house at 136 Potsdamer Strasse, just before it was pulled down.

M.V.S. (E. Müller), water-coloured pen-and-ink drawing, before 1877

duction of rail traffic, as the overwhelming part of the rapidly growing passenger traffic to central, southern and western German countries and abroad in these directions went through the Potsdamer Tor "needle's eye".

And Potsdamer Platz was also more at the centre of attention in terms of local traffic. Private and public hackney carriage traffic was increasing by leaps and bounds. On 30 October 1846 the "Concessionierte Berliner Omnibus Compagnie" was the first horse bus company to be granted a licence for a service in the residence city, and this covered five routes at one go. Three of these ran through Potsdamer Platz: Alexanderplatz–Bendlerstrasse, Carlsbad–Jannowitzbrücke and Anhalter Bahnhof–Schönhauser Tor. Potsdamer Platz was dominated by horse-bus public transport for almost two decades. A licence for a horse tram from Potsdamer Platz to Schöneberg was in fact issued in 1865, but nothing ever came of it.

The establishment of the Potsdam and Anhalt rail services was only the beginning of a development in the course of which Berlin rapidly became an internationally important railway junction.

Berlin's first railway station building was the terminus for the Berlin–Potsdam Railway, which started running in 1838. All Berlin's early railway stations were termini, as they were starting points for independent railways belonging to different companies.

Julius Henning/Carl Schulin, steel engraving, aquatint, 1839

Lines to Stettin (1842), Frankfurt an der Oder (1842), Hamburg (1846), East Prussia (1861) and Görlitz (1866) linked Berlin with important ports, raw material deposits and economic centres, as well as international railway lines to all points of the compass.

The further fate of Potsdamer Platz was influenced for two decades by traffic on a railway line opened in October 1851, intended to bring together important goods traffic from railway companies that were independent of each other. It crossed all the streets and squares at street level along the old excise wall and soon turned out to be a much disliked traffic hazard in Potsdamer Platz as well.

The actor Hugo Wauer was living in Berlin at the time and drew a friend's attention to this precarious situation: "… now just imagine that our child of sorrows the passage through Potsdamer Platz is daily blocked completely six or eight times by a train of 60 to 100 goods wagons driven with the utmost caution for safety reasons and preceded by a railway official pacing as slowly as possible and ringing a large bell, but not 'in the year dot', but even after 1870. And every time one of these trains passes there is a build-up of hundreds of vehicles and thousands of hurrying passers-by." This condition persisted until 1871, when goods traffic between the individual railway companies was shifted on to the new ring railway. It went round the city as it was then in a broad arc.

Berlin situation plan Sineck, Verlag Dietrich Reimers, 1874 (detail)

The excise wall in the area of the square has been pulled down, and the rail link in the new Königgrätzer Strasse was replaced by horse trams in 1851. Two kinds of building are predominant in the area: an unbroken run of residential blocks in Potsdamer and Königgrätzer Strasse and between the Potsdam and Anhalt stations; the villa building style around the St. Matthäikirche up to Tiergarten- and Bellevuestrasse ("Millionaires' Quarter"). The ground plan of Potsdamer Platz is complete and will change in future only as a result of plot development with ever larger and more pompous buildings.

*Peripheral building on the
northern side of Leipziger
Platz. On the left is the little
gatehouse, on the right the
beginning of Leipziger Strasse.*

*Anonymous, tinted pencil
drawing, c. 1860*

26

View of Leipziger Strasse from Leipziger Platz. The traffic is large-ly made up of horse buses and hackney carriages. The corner build-ing designed by Friedrich Hitzig housed the English embassy until 1878, then the Turkish embassy. It had to give way to Alfred Messel's new building for the Wertheim department store in 1896.

W. Loeillot, colour lithograph, c. 1850

Great changes occurred in the design of buildings around Potsdamer Platz after the emergence of the railways. Even after the opening of the line from Berlin to Potsdam the area, as long as the occasional large building was overlooked, was something of a rural idyll. The doctor and journalist Dr. Isidor Kastan, later to live in Victoriastrasse, remembered this state of affairs very vividly:

"The area further westwards, from the beginning of Potsdamer Strasse to the Landwehrkanal, was dominated by a truly peaceful silence, which increased with every step towards the west ... All the houses had broad front gardens, guaranteeing a cosy look with their somewhat folksy arrangements of flowers and arbours, reminiscent of a small town. The 'Sommersche Salon' at 9 Potsdamer Strasse, with a large garden behind it, was universally popular. Here Liebig's 'Symphoniekapelle' played every Wednesday and Saturday; at that time it was the only one in Berlin with an exclusively classical repertoire. ... Apart from the sociable life and activity in 'Sommers Salon' and its adjacent garden everything in Potsdamer Strasse was so quiet and tranquil at that time."

This suburban idyll was now increasingly frequently interrupted by the noise of building as the surroundings of Potsdamer Platz were gradually built up. Fanny Lewald, a writer from Königsberg and a pioneer of the women's emancipation movement moved to Berlin in 1842, where her home was rapidly transformed into a popular literary salon. She described the situation as it was a number of years later:

"In 1840, if one visited the districts around the Potsdamer Thor, it was as lonely there as in Darmstadt or Karlsruhe. The Anhalt railway and the rail routes that had been further opened up from Potsdam attracted hordes of people and traffic to the western end of the city. There were new streets there, like Anhalter Strasse and Askanischer Platz; the whole area between Askanischer Platz and Potsdamer Strasse was a building site. New buildings were going up around the Thiergarten, and they showed a lavishness and taste that would previously never have been dreamt of for private buildings. There had been a striking increase in luxury everywhere."

The first part of Fanny Lewald's description relates to development of the area between the Potsdam and Anhalt stations. Here the street façades were being completed with three- to four-storey residential blocks as a coherent and compact development. Similar building was taking place in Hirschelstrasse and Köthener Strasse, Dessauer and Bernburger Strasse – new in 1844 – and also in Link-, Eichhorn- and Schellingstrasse between the Potsdam railway land and Potsdamer Strasse which latter was also acquiring a completed façade.

On the western side of Potsdamer Strasse building developments were very different. The first building to emerge was the St. Matthäikirche, a church built from 1844 to 1846 by Schinkel's pupil Friedrich August Stüler (1800–1865), and Regenten-, Matthäikirch- and Sigismundstrasse as well as Margarethen- and Victoriastrasse had been laid out around it. The plots were almost all acquired by high financiers. The work of many well-known architects produced a villa quarter of an extraordinarily high architectural standard from 1850. The stylistic spectrum of the houses ran from late neoclassical to historicist forms. Versatile architect Friedrich Hitzig (1811–1881) showed great merit in opening up and developing Victoriastrasse; he adapted the austere country house style of the first decades of the century to the demands of the moneyed aristocracy by using a more elaborate formal language and more meaningful functional design, thus taking villa architecture to an important high point. Bellevue- and Tiergartenstrasse also acquired palace-like residences for millionaires after that. It was no coincidence that this whole area south of the Tiergarten became known as the "Millionaires' Quarter" in the late 19th century. The names of the bankers who had lived or still lived there at that time had an impressive resonance within the business world: Hansemann, Magnus, Fürstenberg, Pinkus, Oppenheim, Gelpcke, Lachmann, Goldschmidt, Simon, Heymann, Rothschild, Schwabach, Wallich – to name only the best known.

Alongside high-grade civil servants and officers like von Jagow, Director Michelet, von Kusserow, Abeken, von Manteuffel, Dr. Lasker, General Graf von Brandenburg and Lieutenant-Colonel Graf Schwerin the large number of well-known academics is also striking: Professors Bardeleben, Magnus, Weierstraß, Gneist, Virchow, Curtius, the brothers Grimm, Droysen and many others lived here. Important artists were also represented, like painters Meyerheim, Hennig, Timm and Begas.

One of the 1848 revolutionaries lived at 26 Potsdamer Strasse: Franz Duncker (1822–1888), who ran his publishing house there, which produced a large number of books of a bourgeois-democratic or liberal-minded nature. He also published Karl Marx's "Critique of Political Economy" in 1859. Incidentally, he also knew one of the other "48ers", who became world-famous as a workers' leader in the early 1860s: Ferdinand Lassalle (1825–1864). Lassalle lived at 13 Bellevuestrasse, where he lived "as luxuriously as his opposite, the

rich man"; at least this was the perception of Karl Marx, who was expelled from Prussia in 1849 and visited Lassalle at home in spring 1861, in a letter to Friedrich Engels dated 10 May of that year.

The district outside the Potsdamer Tor acquired a new main road in 1867, when the old excise wall was pulled down. The modest streets that led along the inside and outside of the wall now formed a single, broad sweep, running from Hallesches Tor via the Potsdamer Tor to the Brandenburger Tor. It now linked important main roads out of the city centre and had a linking function as a mediator between the old town and the new districts that were coming into being. In 1872 it acquired a connection to Wilhelmstrasse north of Leipziger Platz, when Voßstrasse cut through the garden of the late General Graf von Voß-Buch. A second connection of this kind was built south of Anhaltische Strasse, Hedemannstrasse, named after Berlin mayor Heinrich Hedemann (1800–1872).

*The villa at 2 Königgrätzer Strasse, built for mechanical engineering manufacturer Friedrich Wöhlert to plans by architect August Orth.
The proud owner poses for his architect's camera by the garden fence.*

August Orth, 1873

This villa-style residence at 37 Victoriastrasse dates from the first development phase and was once the property of businessman and town councillor Adolph Meyer. It was hemmed in by modern rented accommodation from the turn of the century.

Anonymous, 1910

Something else special had happened to Potsdamer Platz as a result of the demolition of the excise wall: it had opened up to the east. Karl Friedrich Schinkel's little gatehouses had their vestigial walls removed and now, robbed of their original function, stood free in the middle of a large double square, merely as decoration. In fact Leipziger Platz, designed so punctiliously by early 18th century architects, and Potsdamer Platz, which simply continued growing all on its own, in a wild and unruly fashion, were one square from this time onwards. It was still on the periphery of the city, but through its railways above all it was in many ways Berlin's gateway to the world. And it was the centre of the new Tiergarten district.

A perfect example of north German station architecture: the Anhalter Bahnhof, a railway station, rebuilt from 1876 to 1880 to plans by Franz Schwechten. It replaced older buildings dating from 1841.

Hermann Rückwardt, 1881

The impressive splendour of the old "Millionaires' Quarter": the villa in the foreground at 10 Bellevuestrasse on the corner of Lennéstrasse belonged to Kommerzienrat Isidor Gerson, businessman and Belgian consul. The

"Wrangel" fountain, designed by Hugo Hagen and dedicated in 1876, added to the lustre of this villa quarter.

Friedrich Ferdinand Albert Schwartz, 1876

AN UNCHECKED RISE

The influence of the German unification process on the fate of "Athens on the Spree" shows us how much Berlin at that time was not merely a product of the economic upswing and ultra-rapid development of transport, but also above all of "great politics", and the extent to which Potsdamer Platz shared in these events. In the 1850s and 60s the aristocracy, state bureaucracy, the officer class and "grands" and "petits" bourgeois never lived as close to each other and influenced each other so much as in the area around Potsdamer Platz. The "revolution from above" was not conceived and realized by Bismarck, the "smith of the empire" alone, at the green tables of governments or diplomacy, or for instance merely under the constraint of randomly emerging realities. It was also the result of numerous social encounters, of gentlemen's evenings, dinners and house balls in the smart villas of the Tiergarten district – for example in the home of top banker August von der Heydt (1801–1874), who was a minister for a long period, or banker Adolf Hansemann (1826–1903), or Paul von Schwabach (1867–1939), the partner of Bismarck's banker Gerson Bleichröder, and many others. As Carl Fürstenberg (1850–1933), who became the probably most outstanding German banker and later moved into a villa in Victoriastrasse himself, recorded in his memoirs, "numerous personalities close to the court" appeared "at such evenings. ... A large proportion of the diplomatic corps was represented, also ministers, high officials and a large number of elegant officers ..."

After social preparation of this kind, German unity was completed on the battlefields in the "Wars of Unification" with "blood and iron" (Bismarck).

For the subsequent fate of Potsdamer Platz it was not so important that Hirschel- and Schulgartenstrasse, in connection with the demolition of the excise wall, were named Königgrätzer Strasse a year later in memory of the first decisive battle of Königgrätz (3 July 1866), or that annual memorial celebrations of the Prussian victory at Sedan were held in the square itself for many years from 2 September 1871. It was of far greater consequence that at this time Wilhelm- and Leipziger Strasse and Leipziger Platz became the government centre of the North German Alliance and finally of the German Empire.

A process that had already started in the first half of the century now reached its peak: the overwhelming number of German imperial departments, Prussian state authorities and their most important sub-departments had established themselves in 13 buildings in Leipziger Strasse and Leipziger Platz and 13 more in Wilhelmstrasse, mainly in important historical palaces from 1883 onwards. The number of official political and administrative trips, diplomatic missions and finally court and state visits from all over the world that arrived via the Potsdam or the even more prestigious Anhalt station to be received in the Berlin Schloß and conduct negotiations in one of the ministries behind Potsdamer Platz was constantly on the increase.

They included members of the Reichstag, for as soon as the North German Alliance was founded in 1867 its parliament had to be accommodated. The palace at 3 Leipziger Strasse was lighted upon. It had been built in 1737 under the Prussian lieutenant Johann Heinrich von der Groeben, later became Ernst Gotzkowsky's silk factory, was the home of the Mendelssohn-Bartholdy family of bankers and artists until 1851 and then the

Leipziger Platz. Two of the eight statues that used to stand at the corners of the Octogon. They were originally made by sculptor Meyer in the 18th century as lantern-bearers for the bridge over the fortress moat in front of the Royal Opera House in Unter den Linden. The statues came to their new site when Schinkel redesigned the area around the Neue Wache in 1824. They were destroyed with the square in the Second World War.

Georg Bartels, 1903

33

The Prussian Ministry of
Agriculture was opened
at 9/10 Leipziger Platz in
1876 and extended into the

adjacent buildings numbers
6 to 8 in 1890.

Max Missmann, 1910

Prussian Herrenhaus (Upper House). The constituting Reichstag began its session with the sitting
on 25 March 1867. Later the Herrenhaus of the
Landtag sat in this building again, until moving
into Friedrich Schulze's (1843–1912) prestigious
new building, which is still in existence, in 1904.

The parliament for the empire that had come into
being in 1871 was much larger and also needed a
larger building. Bismarck personally evicted the
Royal Porcelain Manufactory from 4 Leipziger
Strasse and had its buildings converted as "interim
premises" to designs by Friedrich Hitzig under the
direction of Gropius & Schmieden. This remained
parliament's home for 23 years, until Paul Wallot
(1841–1912) was able to hand over his highly
controversial and spectacular building by the
Brandenburger Tor in 1894. The great oratorical
duel between Bismarck (1815–1898), Bebel
(1840–1913), Lasker (1829–1884) and many
others in the Reichstag off Leipziger Platz was
the talk of the town.

Victory in the war against France in 1870/71 and
German unification had some other consequences
for Berlin and Potsdamer Platz. The reparations
extorted from France to the tune of 5 billion gold
francs caused an economic boom in Germany
that was of a speculative nature from the start.
Berlin, the new imperial city, was stretching and
extending itself, and putting everything that had
happened until then in the shade. And even its
earlier population growth figures had been impressive: it rose from 192,971 in 1840 to 774,498
in 1870. Moabit, Wedding and Gesundbrunnen
had become heavily populated industrial and workers' residential quarters outside the town gates to
the north and north-east, with 30,000 inhabitants.
They had been incorporated into Berlin as early
as 1861.

Leipziger Platz with the development on its south-western periphery. Buildings in Potsdamer Platz can be seen behind Karl Friedrich Schinkel's gatehouses. The layout of the fenced green space is fundamentally still the same as Peter Joseph Lenné's 1828 design. In the bay on the central promenade is the Hugo Hagen's memorial to the former Prussian prime minister Graf Brandenburg, dedicated in 1862. Opposite, concealed by the trees, it is balanced by the memorial to Field-Marshal von Wrangel, modelled by Karl Keil and dedicated in 1880.

Georg Bartels, 1900

This palace at 102 Wilhelmstrasse was built in 1737 for
Baron Vernezobre, and was
converted for Prince Albrecht
of Prussia by Karl Friedrich
Schinkel from 1830 to 1833.
The "Prinz-Albrecht-Palais"
acquired depressing fame in
the Nazi period: in 1934 it
became the headquarters of
Reinhard Heydrich, director
of the security service (SD)
under the leader of the SS,
and his successor, Ernst
Kaltenbrunner.

Phototype after photograph
by Rammler & Jonas, 1890

The Reichskanzlerpalais
at 77 Wilhelmstrasse was
built as a palace for Graf
Schulenburg in 1736. Princes
Ferdinand and Heinrich of
Prussia lived in it for a time.
Fürst Radziwill acquired it in
1795, from 1876 to 1890 it
was Imperial Chancellor Fürst
Bismarck's residence.

*Photographische Gesellschaft,
1878*

Courtyard of the Royal
Porcelain Manufactory at
4 Leipziger Strasse. Friedrich
Hitzig, with Gropius &
Schmieden converted the
company's front building as a
meeting-place for the Reichstag from 1871. This "provisional arrangement" lasted for
23 years, as Paul Wallot's new
Reichstag building behind the
Brandenburger Tor was not
available for dedication until
1894.

Friedrich Ferdinand Albert
Schwartz, 1888

The old territorial reserve armoury was at 122 Königgrätzer Strasse. The picture shows the courtyard side. The new building for the General Military Paymaster's Office was built in its stead from 1881 to 1883.

Friedrich Ferdinand Albert Schwartz, 1880

The Prussian Chamber of Deputies in Prinz-Albrecht-Strasse was built from 1892 to 1897 to plans by Friedrich Schulze, and was the meeting-place of the Prussian parliament. The German Communist Party was founded in the ballroom at the turn of 1918/19, in 1934/35 the building housed the People's Court, and after that it was the "Airmen's House". From 1961 it was near the Wall, and not accessible to the public.

Max Missmann, 1911

Decorations for Potsdamer Platz on the occasion of the entry of the Prussian troops into Berlin after the war against France on 16 June 1871. They marched along Potsdamer Strasse and across Potsdamer Platz, through Königgrätzer Strasse and the Brandenburger Tor to the Lustgarten. Germania is enthroned above artillery won in battles from the beaten enemy.

Georg Schucht, 1871

41

View into Leipziger Strasse. The left-hand street façade contains the Reichstag at no. 4, the Herrenhaus at no. 3 and at no. 1/2 the Ministry of Trade, which moved here in 1887. In the background are Leipziger Platz and buildings in Potsdamer Platz, with an advertisement for court photographer Friedrich Ferdinand Albert Schwartz, who lived at the corner of Bellevuestrasse from 1887 to 1902 and had a studio there.

Friedrich Ferdinand Albert Schwartz, 1892

Former palace of the Mendelssohn-Bartholdy family of bankers and artists at 3 Leipziger Strasse. It was converted for use as a meeting-place for the Herrenhaus in 1851, and the parliament of the North German Alliance met here from 1867–1870. Adjacent on the left is the former Royal Porcelain Manufactory, "provisional" meeting-place of the German parliament from 1871. *Friedrich Ferdinand Albert Schwartz, 1882*

Potsdam Bridge. View north
into Potsdamer Strasse.
Typical late 19th century tene-
ment building with façades in
the post-Schinkel classical
style (late classicism).

Georg Bartels, May 1897

44

Potsdam Bridge over the Landwehrkanal marks the point at which the Potsdamer Chaussee with its turning to Leipzig passed the Schafgraben in its day. In 1897/98 it was rebuilt with Victoria Bridge as a joint iron arched bridge, under city architect Fr. Eiselen. The effective craftsmanship of the furnishing was artistically rounded off with four bronze groups by Reinhold Felderhoff, Jaensch, Max Klein and Julius Moser.

Hermann Rückwardt, 1899

This late neo-classical villa
dating from before 1870 belonged to legal councillor and
city councillor Carl Eduard
Dircksen. It is flanked by turn-
of-the-century blocks of flats.

Georg Bartels, 1903

46

View from Potsdamer Platz into Potsdamer Strasse. Theodor Fontane lived at no. 134c in the seventh building on the left after the junction with Linkstrasse.

Georg Bartels, 1897

This had happened in this context at the same time as a more densely occupied part of the Schöneberg area south of the Landwehrkanal, which meant that the Berlin boundary was pushed beyond the Botanical Gardens.

A sea of buildings built in various ways and for very different functions, of varying quality and greater and lesser degrees of comfort, with occupants of all classes and levels, this and that professional group had grown up, contradictorily but powerfully, in the area around Potsdamer Platz – belonging to various independent local administrative authorities, but already a town, not yet Berlin,

Potsdamer Strasse, once built up with garden houses and villas, has lost its semi-rural character and has become the metropolis's main thoroughfare. Blocks of flats at the corner of Eichhornstrasse. Georg Bartels, 1897

but absorbed in a variety of ways into the functional structure of this imperial and now cosmopolitan city. And at the centre of all this was Potsdamer Platz: even in its immediate vicinity it was possible to see the increasing density of the population. The same area in which we counted 439 families of tenants and owners in 1836 had 4,384 in 1883. Among these the 843 families of bankers, brokers, money-changers and persons of private income were the most numerous, then came 815 businessmen and their families, 734 craftsmen, 633 low-grade civil servants, 230 high-grade civil servants and 200 officers and their families; all the other professions were represented by fewer than 200 families.

Comparison with the 1836 figures shows that the same six professional groups top the list , but there have been some changes in the order: bankers and stockbrokers, estate agents, money changers and merchants are now well ahead of the civil servants. The "Privy Councillors' Quarter" was now more often popularly called the "Millionaires' Quarter".

A square whose surrounding population equalled that of a small town, crossed by thousands of travellers and tourists daily, used as a route from the east of the town to the west and vice versa, a square like that needed to have better transport access. First the Potsdam and Anhalt stations acquired prestigious large-scale facilities. The new Potsdam station was built from 1868 to 1872 under the direction of L. Quassowski, in brick; the bottom section and decorative elements were in weatherproof sandstone. Architect Franz Schwechten (1841–1924) used the highest architectural standards for the new Anhalt station, built from 1876 to 1880. This brick building in a pleasing arched style, decorated with moulded bricks and terra cotta and completed with sand-

stone sections was and is considered by architectural critics to be the high point of 19th century Berlin station art.

Both buildings had spacious ticket halls and waiting rooms, with classes 1 to 4 strictly separated, and also special reception and rest rooms for the royal or imperial court, which were also used for important state receptions. Receptions of this kind with their pomp and circumstance made more impact on everyday events in Potsdamer Platz than the continuous mass arrival of mainly nameless passengers that flooded into the streets and squares from the increasingly frequent trains, a phenomenon that had swiftly been accepted. The two oldest Berlin stations maintained their dominance for passenger traffic in particular: in 1890/91 for example 1,473,819 passengers travelled from the Potsdam station and 1,238,051 from the Anhalt station, far more than from other stations in the city.

View of the new Potsdamer Bahnhof, built to plans by L. Quassowski and dedicated in 1872. Behind the wall by the parked hackney carriages is the old cemetery of the Trinity parish.

Max Missmann, 1910

Top left: State reception at the Anhalter Bahnhof. The new Chinese ambassador, General Yintchang, has arrived.

Gebrüder Haeckel, 1908

Bottom left: The Potsdamer Bahnhof also had famous passengers. Imperial Chancellor Fürst von Bülow gets into a hackney carriage after leaving the station.

Gebrüder Haeckel, 1908

The south façade of Pots-
damer Platz. On the left is the
new Hotel Fürstenhof building,
built 1906/07 to plans by
Reichenberg & Moser, with
Café Fürstenhof and the

Leipziger Hof beer restaurant.
Potsdamer Bahnhof is flanked
by Konditorei Telschow.

Max Missmann, 1907

View of development on the
south-western periphery of
Potsdamer Platz. From left to
right one can make out the
Hotel Fürstenhof, Potsdamer
Bahnhof, the Pschorr-Bräu-
Haus with Konditorei

Telschow in the next building
and beyond that the junction
with Linkstrasse. On the
right-hand edge of the picture
is Café Josty's front garden.

Max Missmann, 1925

51

After the link line had been removed in 1871 it was possible to adapt the local transport system centred on Potsdamer Platz to the increased demand. Horse-drawn trams conquered the terrain. A contract had been signed for such a system as early as 1865 – the year in which the first Berlin horse-tram was born. The route was intended to serve Schöneberg, but construction was continually postponed. So it was not until 1873, after the excise wall had been pulled down and the removal of the link line, that the first horse-tram route started to operate from the Potsdamer Tor to Hallesches Tor. The "Große Berliner Pferdeeisenbahn AG" ("Great Berlin Horse-Railway Company") then at last opened the line from Potsdamer Platz to Schöneberg, and it was soon extended to Spittelmarkt. This line soon came to be the busiest in Berlin. Then things moved faster and faster, and the increasing traffic in Potsdamer Platz fascinated visitors to the Residence in particular. And so Theodor Fontane had his General Poggenpuhl, who had once more fled the tranquillity of his estate to pay a visit to Berlin, look out of his window in the Fürstenhof Hotel and say to himself:

"… quite frankly, I prefer Potsdamer Platz, because there is most life there. And life is the best thing a big city has … and when I lie down by the window there in the mornings, with a sofa cushion under both my arms, and fresh winter air is blowing across from Hallesches Tor … and I have the Bellevue and Josty cafés before me, Josty with the glazed veranda, where there are people sitting reading newspapers from an early hour, and horse-trams and buses coming in from all directions, and looking as though they're going to collide at any moment, and the flower-girls amidst it all … and in all that noise and confusion there are shouts of extra editions – children, if I remember rightly, then I feel contented, then I know that I am among people again, and that's something I wouldn't like to give up."

The rapid expansion of the inner-city and western-suburban horse-tram network made Potsdamer Platz with its popular Potsdam, Anhalt, Wannsee and Ringbahn stations into Berlin's most important traffic junction. In about 1895 there was nowhere else in the town to match Potsdamer Platz's 244 horse-trams travelling in all directions every hour of the day. Electrification of the trams did not really get going in this area until 1900, but it was as early as 21 August 1902 that the last inner-city horse-tram ran from Großgörschenstrasse via Potsdamer Platz to Wedding. Two years later there were 34 tram routes crossing the square, and still six horse-bus routes. The picture is completed by heavy hackney carriage traffic. In high summer, the "high season", an average of 343 hackney carriages came from or to the Potsdamer Bahnhof, and even 361 from or to the Anhalter Bahnhof.

But noises were starting up underground as well. The Berliners were unused to this kind of building: streets were excavated to a depth of several metres to create a tunnel for the "under-pavement railway", and Berlin's first underground station

Remains of the excise wall a the junction with Prinz-Albrecht-Strasse. The circle of this last Berlin "city wall", which at first consisted partly of wooden palisades, had enclosed the town until 1737. The Potsdamer Tor was one of the 15 town gates. Demolition of the wall started in 1867.

Otto Hasselkampf, 1901

was the one by the main-line Potsdamer Bahnhof. And so this was connected to the first overhead and underground railway line form the start; it ran from the Warschauer Brücke to the Knie station, and was opened in 1902.

Fontane's old Poggenpuhl discovered another special feature of the Potsdamer Platz area from his hotel window: cafés, wine bars and restaurants, of which there were many other than Bellevue and Josty. And a stroll would show you an illustrious clientele. Perhaps Anton von Werner (1843–1915), the painter, or Begas and Kaulbach. They all lived in this area. The famous Adolf Menzel (1815 –1905) crops up in almost all legends and reminiscences about this quarter. He had worked his way up into the front rank of Berlin painters – sometimes painting and drawing with both hands, it was said – and popular in all circles of the population. Banker Carl Fürstenberg, who often enough observed this little great man outside his villa in Victoriastrasse, describes his appearance:

"Even towards the turn of the century a small excellency with a large, interesting head, framed by a little round beard, was a familiar sight in west Berlin, where he used to walk from Margarethen-strasse along Victoriastrasse to the Tiergarten at the same time every day."

Other chroniclers saw him as a regular in various inns, for example every evening in the Frederich wine bar at 12 Potsdamer Strasse, where the land-lord is said to have fixed a coat-hook in such a way that the great master could still reach it from his diminutive height. Or perhaps in Weinhaus Huth, established in Linkstrasse in 1871, and also fre-quented by Heinrich Seidel (1842–1906). He was just as well known as an engineer for his highly individual hall roof structure for the Anhalter

Bahnhof as for his "Vorstadtgeschichten" ("Sub-urban Stories"; 1880) or the story "Leberecht Hühnchen" ("Liveright Chicken"; 1882); the author Gustav Freytag is said to have been seen here regularly as well.

But he not infrequently saw Theodor Fontane (1819–1898) here too; he lived from 1873 till his death at 134c Potsdamer Strasse. He was already widely known as a journalist and writer, but he wrote his important social novels in these sur-roundings, with a keen eye for people, things and events. No wonder that the Potsdamer Platz area appears as the background to his character's actions in many of his realistic narratives. For example, the description of the weekly market that has now made a site on the edge of Potsdamer Platz its own, can be experienced down to the last detail in his novel "Cécile" (1885).

Potsdamer Platz is connected to the first Berlin underground and overhead railway line, which opened in 1902. Tunnel works by the railway station building. Buildings in König-grätzer Strasse can be seen in the background.

Anonymous, 1901

Frederich's Hotel at 12 Pots-
damer Strasse, one of the
most popular wine bars in this
area. Theodor Fontane and
Adolf Menzel were regulars
here.

Hugo Rudolphy, c. 1890

54

Konditorei Telschow in Potsdamer Platz. As the Pschorr-
Bräu-Haus beer palace is to
be sited here Telschow is
advertising its move into the
next-door building. On the
left there is a view into

Königgrätzer Strasse, and on
the right the junction with
Potsdamer Strasse can be
made out.

Hugo Rudolphy, 1909

The north side of Potsdamer
Platz, bordered by the group
of buildings between Königgrätzer Strasse and Leipziger
Tor with the Palasthotel.

Friedrich Ferdinand Albert
Schwartz, 1890

View of building on the northern periphery of Potsdamer Platz. From left to right Café Josty and Bellevuestrasse, the Hotel Bellevue, built by Ludwig Heim 1887/88 and Königgrätzer Strasse, next to it the Palasthotel, rebuilt and extended by Ludwig Heim 1892/93.

Max Missmann, 1910

Following double page: On the left between the two gatehouses is Leipziger Strasse. On the right-hand side, the view south into Königgrätzer Strasse from Potsdamer Platz shows on the left the new Hotel Fürstenhof building. The Völkerkunde-museum (ethnology museum) can be seen at the end of the group of buildings in front of the Prinz-Albrecht-Palais garden.

Max Missmann, 1907

Prinz-Albrecht-Strasse. View of the Kunstgewerbemuseum (arts and crafts museum), built 1872 to 1881 to plans by Martin Gropius and Heino Schmieden ("Martin-Gropius-Bau"). Next to it is the Arts *and Crafts library building.*

Max Missmann, 1907

60

"… which, as usual, was held at this point between the roadway and the house-fronts. Here the market women sat almost as if on parade 'wedged into a fearful strait'. … For yards around containers of raspberries were arranged along the pavement, interrupted only by tall, pannier-like baskets, with bilberries peeping out of them, blue-black and still with a hint of bloom as a sign of their freshness. But in the forefront, as specially magnificent items, were shapeless late giant strawberries on box and crate lids, and between them were great bundles of cornflowers and poppies, wallflowers and for-get-me-nots as well, with long strings of raffia, so that the flowers could be made into a bouquet if wished."

Given such rapid population growth and the rapidly increasing number of travellers, above all tourists, the question of catering repeatedly arose. In 1883 the area between Tiergartenstrasse, Land-wehrkanal, Bendlerstrasse and Potsdamer Platz was already very well provided for, with 92 restaurants, 10 spirits bars, 13 Viennese cafés and cake-shops and 36 public houses. There are some famous names on the list: Café Josty, which had moved from the city centre in 1880, Frederich and Aschinger in Potsdamer Strasse, Fürstenberg in Askanischer Platz, Telschow in Potsdamer Platz and Westphal in Königgrätzer Strasse and … and … The luxury hotels dating from the turn of the century all offered fine restaurants and prestigious cafés as well, of course.

As well as all this, the period around 1900 pro-duced innovations in this field as well: the catering profession's great beer and wine houses on a completely new scale, palaces to meet mass re-quirements, as it were. Between 1901 and 1912 the following establishments appeared one after the other: the Münchner Königliches Hofbräuhaus at 127/28 Potsdamer Strasse, the Alt-Bayern, 10/11 Potsdamer Strasse, Weinhaus Rheingold, 3 Potsdamer Strasse, 19/20 Bellevuestrasse, Bier-haus Siechen, 3 Potsdamer Platz and Weinhaus Huth, 139 Potsdamer Strasse, 45 Linkstrasse. The monumental "Alt-Bayern" beer palace, offered to the amazed public by architect Wilhelm Walther (1857–1917) showed very clearly that it is possible to drink even beer in a cultural way. The various public rooms, halls and courtyards (did anyone ever count them?) were designed with all the re-finements that Romanesque, Gothic, Renaissance and Baroque design had to offer. The lavishly de-signed interiors used the most exquisite materials, tiles, marble, noble woods, gilded and silvered stucco ceilings, ceramics and glass mosaics; and from façades, paintings and niches German prin-ces, kings and emperors, saints and artists seemed to be nodding to the beer-drinkers, and – Kaiser Wilhelm II in oil.

"Haus Potsdam", built to designs by Franz Schwechten in Königgrätzer Straße between Köthener Strasse and the Potsdamer Bahnhof in 1911/12 presented its restaurants, cinema, offices but above all the two storeys of its Café Piccadilly in precisely the right way. This latter was just as luxuriously decorated and furnished, but less patriotic than "Alt-Bayern", and so when the First World War broke out it had to abandon its un-German name, apparently wounding to na-tional feelings, and was called "Café Vaterland" from then on. Thus Potsdamer Platz and the sur-rounding area had a great deal to offer after the turn of the century in this respect as well.

A square that was the lively link between the old town and the newer districts, centre of an empire, flanked by two cosmopolitan railway stations, a centre with numerous sights, is predestined

*Light well of the Kunst-
gewerbemuseum (arts and
crafts musem) in Prinz-
Albrecht-Strasse.*

Lorenz Ritter, etching, no year

to become the centre for visitors' accommodation as well. The early stages of this could be seen even when its peripheral position attracted Berliners and visitors who wanted to enjoy the natural idyll of "God's free nature" away from the centre of the city for more than just one day. The 1836 directory recorded twelve inn-keepers, hoteliers and boarding-house owners for the area around Potsdamer Platz.

By 1883 the picture was fundamentally different. Now there were already twelve real hotels here, several of them of international standard, like Hotel Fürstenhof at 2 Leipziger Platz, Hotel du Parc at 11 Königgrätzer Strasse, Hotel Askanischer Hof at 21 Königgrätzer Strasse, the Westendhotel at 23 Königgrätzer Strasse, the Hotel Gericke

at 3 Bahnhofstrasse or the Hotel Sanssouci at 12 Linkstrasse. But the growing metropolis with its increasing tourist industry made ever greater demands. New large hotels, the majority in the emerging style of the luxury metropolitan hotel, were built around the Potsdamer Tor, as in other parts of Berlin; the Bellevue Hotel in 1887/88 and the Palasthotel in 1892/93 in Potsdamer Platz; the Hotel Esplanade in Bellevuestrasse in 1907/08, Hotel Fürstenhof in Königgrätzer Strasse and Leipziger Platz in 1906/07 and the Hotel Exzelsior in Königgrätzer Strasse in 1908.

Of course it was not just stations, new luxury accommodation, hotels, beer, wine and coffee houses that were built in that half-century that made Potsdamer Platz really world-famous.

The Völkerkundemuseum
(ethnology museum),
Königgrätzer Strasse/corner
of Prinz-Albrecht-Strasse was
built 1881–1885 by Ende
& Kluthmann. Next to it on
the left are the Kunstgewerbemuseum (arts and crafts
museum) and library.

Max Missmann, 1907

63

The state commissioned some buildings that fitted in with the area's functional diversity but also had an effect on its architecture. The Kunstgewerbe-museum (arts and crafts museum) was built from 1872 to 1881 to plans by Gropius and Schmieden, a building from the younger Schinkel school designed like a palazzo. It was lavishly decorated and furnished, because it wanted its architecture as well as its contents to demonstrate all arts and crafts techniques and also contemporary technical possibilities. The massive rotunda of the Museum für Völkerkunde (ethnology museum) was built immediately adjacent to it to plans by Hermann Ende from 1880 to 1886 and the Kunstgewerbeschule, the arts and crafts educational establishment, on the Wilhelmstrasse side from 1901 to 1905.

Another major influence on the architecture in the area around Potsdamer and Leipziger Platz were

two new buildings for the Prussian parliament, designed by architect Friedrich Schulze. The Prussian Chamber of Deputies (Preußisches Abge-ordnetenhaus) was built opposite the Kunstgewer-bemuseum from 1892 to 1898, and Prinz-Albrecht-Strasse was laid out between these two buildings as a connection with Königgrätzer Strasse. The new Herrenhaus with its massive façade on Leipziger Strasse was completed by 1904.

And so all in all Potsdamer Platz had developed on a somewhat exaggerated scale. It first appeared in the 19th century as a relatively insignificant square on the periphery of the royal residence. Berlin's rise to cosmopolitan status was reflected in the history of the square. And so it completed its transition into the twentieth century as the central square in an enormously expanded city, as a link between old and new Berlin, and as this city's gateway to the rest of Germany, and to a certain extent to the world.

BETWEEN THE WARS

The First World War, the post-war crisis and the period of inflation subdued the turbulent life and action around Potsdamer Platz. Of course it remained the traffic centre of the capital, and when Greater Berlin was formed on 1 October 1920 it moved from the periphery of the city to the centre in administrative terms as well. But the cosmopolitan element, the ceaseless movement, was missing in those years. The economic depression could be felt more strongly here. But even before the middle of the decade an upturn began that went into history as the "Golden Twenties". Even those who didn't get their hand on much of this gold could bask in its glow in Potsdamer Platz, even if only as an onlooker.

Berlin

Dessin 5

Potsdamer Platz

*Potsdamer Platz. North side
with Hotel Bellevue,
Königgrätzer Strasse and
the Palasthotel.*

*Postcard photograph, partially
coloured, c. 1905*

Potsdamer Platz.

Postcard photograph, partially
coloured, c. 1900

Potsdamer Platz.
Views of the Potsdamer Bahn-
hof, Café Josty and Leipziger
Strasse.

Colour lithograph (postcard),
c. 1900

Potsdam Square. *Potsdamerplatz.* *Place de Potsdam.*

Potsdamer Platz.

*Leaf from the "Album von
Berlin Charlottenburg und
Potsdam", c. 1911*

Berlin. Potsdamerplatz. 216.

Potsdamer Platz.

Postcard photograph, partially coloured, c. 1910

BERLIN – Der alte Potsdamer Platz

Potsdamer Platz.

*Coloured postcard photo-
graph and the black-and-
white original, 1933/34*

70

Berlin, Potsdamer Platz

Berlin. Potsdamer Platz

Potsdamer Platz.

Postcard photograph, partially
coloured, c. 1938

In Askanischer Platz.

Special print, coloured subsequently "after a natural coloured photograph", c. 1938

72

This bird's-eye view of Leipziger and Potsdamer Platz shows busy traffic. The peripheral buildings clockwise from the left-hand gatehouse: Hotel Fürstenhof, Königgrätzer Strasse is hidden, Potsdamer Bahnhof, the Pschorr-Bräu-Haus with Konditorei Telschow, Potsdamer Strasse, Café Josty, Bellevuestrasse, Hotel Bellevue, Königgrätzer Strasse, Palasthotel, right-hand gatehouse, Leipziger Strasse.

Aero Lloyd aerial photograph, 1919

View of Potsdamer Platz
during the 1919 transport
strike. Employees being transported by horse-drawn
vehicles.

Anonymous, 1919

74

Indissolubly bound by tradition and function with the old centre, which was increasingly developing into the business, government and cultural centre, Potsdamer Platz now found its hinterland in the "exclusive west", in the Kurfürstendamm, in Tauentzien and Joachimsthaler Strasse; and the "flight" of the rich to the Grunewald and Wannsee assumed "mass" proportions. In compensation, parts of the former "Millionaires' Quarter" became the home and operational field of international diplomacy.

Mobilizing young people for the struggle against the Weimar Republic: Hülsen Free Corps recruiting office in the later "Haus Vaterland".

Willy Römer, 1919

Learning for democracy: training for Berlin works committee members in the Prussian Chamber of Deputies.

W. Gircke, 1919

Potsdam and Anhalt railway facilities. Top left is the Tiergarten. Next to it almost in the centre of the picture are the Potsdamer Bahnhof and Potsdamer and Leipziger Platz. At the top in the centre of the picture are the Anhalter

Bahnhof with Askanischer Platz. From the Brandenburger Tor Königgrätzer Strasse can be seen, leading across Potsdamer Platz and via the Anhalt station to Belle-Alliance-Platz at the top right-hand edge of the picture.

Aero Lloyd aerial photograph, 1919

Potsdamer Platz with view
of Leipziger Strasse. The pen-
tagonal traffic tower with
Germany's first traffic lights
under the roof was built to
regulate the increasingly
problematical traffic mêlée
in 1924.

Max Missmann, 1924

Wertheim department store in
Leipziger Strasse by Leipziger
Platz.

Anonymous, c. 1936

View over the Leipziger Tor to Potsdamer Platz and into Potsdamer Strasse. From left to right Hotel Fürstenhof, the Pschorr-Bräu-Haus, Café Josty and the Hotel Bellevue.

Max Missmann, 1927

79

Life in Potsdamer Platz at this time became more hurried, more turbulent, more extravagant, and the entertainment and tourist industries enjoyed enormous success. This was also expressed in the few important buildings built here at that time. For example in the noble "Café am Tiergarten", 11 Bellevuestrasse, 37 Victoriastrasse, built by architect Oskar Kaufmann (1873–1956), which acquired the exotic name "Mokka Efti" in 1933. Or the "Fürstenbergbräu", 3 Linkstrasse, whose public rooms were designed in rustic Bavarian style. Most clearly recognizable were the heightened ambitions when "Haus Vaterland" was converted in 1928; it was already owned by the Kempinskis. As well as the gigantic Café Vaterland on the ground floor further public rooms were created, with idyllic names like Rheinterrasse, Grinzing, Löwenbräu, Türkisches Café, Wild-West-Bar, Czardas and Mexico-Bar, all decorated appropriately to the countries concerned. There were five kitchens in all, including what was then the largest gas-fuelled kitchen in Europe, suggesting a turnover that was probably unequalled.

The "Europahaus"
palais de danse,
interior and exterior.

Anonymous, 1931

Of course there were developments in fields other than gastronomy, but elsewhere as well. Potsdamer Platz was home to the new Universal-Film AG (UfA) as early as 1917 – it moved into the "Haus Vaterland" office premises. Then a little further on, at 10 Potsdamer Strasse, we find the Vox-Haus, dating from the turn of the century, from which the first radio broadcasts had been conquering the aether and the listeners' hearts since 29 October 1923.

Potsdamer Platz also did full justice to its reputation as a commercial centre in this period. The cosmopolitan setting was changed by fine office and administrative buildings, of which only the two largest are named here. The Europahaus, an administrative and entertainment centre with a 280 m street façade was built in Königgrätzer Strasse, after 1925 called Friedrich-Ebert-Strasse and later south of that Stresemannstrasse. Architects Hans Bielenberg, Josef Moser and Otto Firle were responsible for this copybook example of Neue Sachlichkeit, stepped from twelve to three storeys, with modern offices, several restaurants and cafés, a cinema, a theatre, and the "Tanzpalast" – an essential in the twenties.

Top: A new palace for Gambrinus: the Rheingold wine company took up the whole complex between 3 Potsdamer Strasse and 19/20 Bellevuestrasse.

Max Missmann, 1910

Bottom: The Rheingold wine company illuminated by neon signs.

Anonymous, 1931

Entertainment palace and high-rise office block: this multi-purpose building built between 1911/12 to plans by Franz Schwechten was originally called "Haus Potsdam", and its gigantic café "Piccadilly". At the beginning of the First World War, when the chauvinistic tide was running high, it had to change its name to Vaterland "Deutsches Café-haus" and later to "Café Vaterland".

Max Missmann, 1926

The neon sign decade created a glow of metropolitan light: Kempinski in "Haus Vaterland".

Anonymous, c. 1930

On the afternoon of 2. 7. 1934.
Two days after the Röhm Putsch
traffic in Potsdamer Platz was
back to normal.

Anonymous, 1934

Architect Erich Mendelsohn's (1887–1953) Columbushaus, of the same school but less articulated, was built directly on Potsdamer Platz in 1927. It was a nine-storey office building, dwarfing the buildings in the old development. Impressive differences could be seen in the square after nightfall. The "Golden Twenties" saw the birth of glowing, flickering neon signs, changing from red to blue and green to yellow or white; they made visitors believe that the world is never really beautiful until the evening. Life in Potsdamer Platz was turbulent and intensive – day and night.

Hotel Bellevue had to make way for the Columbushaus in 1927. This was a highly controversial office building by Erich Mendelsohn, which brought "Neue Sachlichkeit" to Potsdamer Platz.

Anonymous, c. 1935

85

The "Europahaus" was built
in Askanischer Platz outside
the Anhalter Bahnhof from
1925 to 1927, as a multi-
purpose building for administration and culture. It con-
tained offices of all kinds,
shops, restaurants and cafés,
a cinema, a cabaret and a
palais de danse.

Max Missmann, 1931

TWELVE YEARS OF MADNESS

After the National Socialist "seizure of power" on 30 January 1933 not much changed at first in Potsdamer Platz. Life was as vibrant as it had ever been. Certainly there were swastika flags everywhere, and men in black and brown uniforms appeared all the more frequently, and finally mysterious figures in dark leather coats became part of this busy scene as well. SS and police vehicles were to be seen more and more often. The Nazis established the headquarters of their oppressive machine close by Potsdamer Platz. Early in May 1933 the head of the Geheime Staatspolizei (Gestapo) Rudolf Diels (later replaced by Reinhard Heydrich) moved into the former arts and crafts school at 8 Prinz-Albrecht-Strasse. The notorious Gestapo prison was set up here in the same year, in which confessions were often extorted by brutal torture and which soon became a transit station to the concentration camps. Later the Reichssicherheitshauptamt (RSAH) also moved into this building. Reinhard Heydrich (1904–1942) also led the SS Security Service (SD), and in this capacity he moved into his headquarters in the Prinz-Albrecht-Palais at 102 Wilhelmstrasse in 1934. The Prussian Chamber of Deputies was also occupied by the new ruler of the state for a time. The notorious People's Court met here from July 1934 to March 1935.

It soon became clear that the Nazi rulers were genuine illusionists and had a great feel for enormous spectacle and the gigantic. State receptions were on the increase: Olympic Games, Berlin's 700th Anniversary, party parades, party rallies in Nuremberg with mass participation from Berlin – the Anhalt and Potsdam stations went through a great period, and on all these occasions the "Imperial Capital" was a mass of flags and banners.

This urge towards the gigantic made itself felt in architecture as well. The most visible proof of this appeared quite close by. The old Reichskanzlerpalais with the Reichskanzlei extension in Wilhelmstrasse dating from 1928 to 1930 did not match Hitler's great urge for power.

For this reason Albert Speer (1905–1988) designed a monstrous Führer palace of enormous dimensions. Stylistically this fitted in with the series of spartan neo-classical buildings of the Nazi period, except that its austerity and emptiness put everything else in the shade. Even before the outbreak of the Second World War Hitler, who already saw himself as leader of a "newly-ordered" Europe, experienced a few "uplifting" moments in his new palace. Even before this Albert Speer had publicly announced his plans for redesigning the imperial capital. Central to this was the north-south axis that cut through Berlin slightly to the west of the Brandenburger Tor and Potsdamer Platz.

Flower stalls outside the Pschorr-Bräu-Haus. In the background are Haus Vaterland and the Potsdamer Bahnhof.

Anonymous, 1936

Building the tunnel for the north-south S-Bahn between Potsdamer Platz and the Brandenburger Tor. A large number of building workers were buried on this stretch on 20 August 1935, and 19 of them lost their lives. The Tiergarten is to the left of Hermann-Göring-Strasse, and on the right are the gardens of the government buildings in Wilhelmstrasse.

Anonymous, 1936

50. H.G.
17.9.36.

Covered excavation ditch for
the north-south S-Bahn tunnel
beyond Potsdamer Platz.
The main building work for
this stretch lasted from 1933
to 1939; it led through the
city centre, running under the

Spree and the Landwehrkanal.

Anonymous, 1936

This led from a new northern station on the ring railway to a south station near Tempelhof airfield, with a "Volkshalle" (People's Hall) for a million people, a triumphal arch and gigantic administrative palaces for government, party and army. Potsdamer Platz would have mouldered away as a result of a new "Runder Platz" (Circular Square) south-west of it. The two traditional stations in Potsdamer and Askanischer Platz would have been made superfluous by a tunnel for rail traffic running under the north-south axis.

One of the many projects that were never realized? Not quite. Building work started in the early years of the war. Surveys were carried out, old buildings were removed, excavations begun and the first new buildings started. The Runder Platz south-west of Potsdamer Platz started to take shape. Everything was hindered by the regime's own policies, which had led to war.

But one more modest but useful project was realized. In May 1933 the Wannsee railway, which ran beside the Potsdam railway facilities, had been electrified. At the same time plans dating from before the First World War to link local trains terminating at the Stettiner Bahnhof and travelling north with those arriving at Potsdamer Platz from the south. Boring work on the tunnel through the city centre started in May 1933. On 20 August 1935 work was interrupted by a tragic accident: the tunnel walls collapsed between the Brandenburger Tor and Potsdamer Platz, and 19 of the buried workers could not be brought out alive. The work, some of which was complicated, dragged on for years. Tunnels had to be built under the Spree and the Landwehrkanal. Potsdamer Platz acquired its station and an intermediate level with access to the north-south railway, the Potsdamer Bahnhof and the U-Bahn (underground), and all this happened without major traffic restrictions. The last section between the Potsdam and Anhalt stations was opened on 9 October 1939. It was now possible to travel north-south on the north-south railway without changing.

Expecting visitors: square outside the Potsdamer Bahnhof before the start of the Olympic Games.

Anonymous, 1936

The end of Albert Speer's "grandiose development plan": a new building for the north-south axis in the Potsdamer Strasse area after devastation in the Second World War.

A. Vennemann, 1948

View of Stresemannstrasse (formerly Königgrätzer Strasse) looking towards the "Haus Vaterland" in July 1945.

Jindřich Marco, 1945

RUBBLE AND ASHES ...

Potsdamer Platz itself had survived the Nazi "peace plan" unscathed. But the war the Nazi rulers had started with the aim of "re-ordering Europe" and dominating the world had affected it severely. Some bombs fell here during the numerous air-raids on Berlin from 1941, damaging or destroying this or that building in Potsdamer Platz. But when carpet bombing started in November 1943 damage became more extensive on each occasion. In January and February, but particularly in April and May 1944 the government quarter was a target for heavy bombing. Potsdamer and Leipziger Platz were now damaged on a catastrophic scale. One of the USAAF's major raids on 3 February 1945 with 937 aircraft almost completely destroyed Potsdamer and Leipziger Platz in just one and a half hours.

When the Americans and Britons stopped bombing Berlin on 21 April 1945 there was scarcely a building in this area that was undamaged. But the attacks ended only because the Allied Red Army had reached Berlin. The Fascist rulers insisted

Stresemannstrasse (formerly Königgrätzer Strasse) in July 1945.

Jindřich Marco, 1945

on continuing their crazy resistance. Units of the Waffen-SS, the Wehrmacht and the Volkssturm stubbornly defended the last positions around the Neue Reichskanzlei and the Führerbunker. Even after several high-placed Nazis had withdrawn from responsibility by committing suicide the struggle had to be continued. Day-long artillery bombardment, air attacks and constant shooting from anti-tank infantry weapons buried what were anyway the pitiful remains of the double square that had once been so cared for and the streets around it in the heart of Berlin under rubble and ashes. As early as 28 April Soviet Army units had reached the Landwehrkanal. There was heavy fighting around Potsdam Bridge, and on 30 April Soviet advance troops occupied parts of Potsdamer Platz.

On 2 May fighting came to an end here as well. Shortly after midnight the German commander of this combat sector sent the following radio signal:

"Hallo, hallo! This is the 56th Panzer Corps. We request a cease-fire. We will send peace negotiators to Potsdam Bridge at nought hours fifty Berlin time."

93

Where plans for conquering the world used to be made: in the courtyard of the Neue Reichskanzlei, a round tower above the Führerbunker.
Anonymous, 1945

Right: Rooms in the former Führerbunker.
Detlev Konnerth, 15. 8. 1990

Here too the war was at an end, but it was indeed "five past twelve": the decision came too late, not just for many people, but for Potsdamer and Leipziger Platz as well. An insatiable mania for world domination had left an immense sea of ruins precisely here, in the once proud, lively centre of the city.

Potsdamer Strasse in July 1945.

Jindřich Marco, 1945

Following double page: On the left is the Leipziger Tor, next to it the Pschorr-Bräu-Haus.

O. Hagemann, 1947

Marking the border between the British and the Soviet sector in Potsdamer Platz.

Henry Ries, 21. 8. 1948

Resurrection or the End?

Many of those returning found "their" Berlin as desolate and depressing as did dramatist and writer Günther Weisenborn (1902–1969). He had been confined in the death cell of Luckau prison as a resistance fighter and freed from there by Soviet soldiers, and soon returned to the city in which he used to work. He stood completely at a loss in Wilhelmstrasse, looking across the Tiergarten to Potsdamer Platz and the west. He remembers his feelings in "Aufzeichnungen eines Außenseiters – Der gespaltene Himmel" (Notes by an Outsider – the Split Sky):

"When I arrived in the city I had not seen for years I stopped for a moment. The enormous city had fallen to its knees like a grey giant, roofs lay on the ground floor, the people wandering around were surrounded by a forest of ruins. ... Remains of net curtains with lazy little bellies wafted out of hollow windows and desolate walls. Or you looked into three flats one on top of the other whose outside wall had fallen away. ... But the most astonishing thing was the silence. This city's millions of people were asleep or moving around softly like mice, colourless and suspicious. You could see a long way. The whole expanse of the Tiergarten was bare and burned. Ruined stone kings lay in the 'plaster avenue'. Other monuments stood in the midday light, farcically mutilated. Now and again a ruined wall fell into the street. From the Brandenburger Tor to Lützowplatz the eye traversed over a hilly desert landscape, and the wind drew veils of brown brick dust, glowing purple in the sun, into the Tiergarten from collapsed tenements and ruined banking temples. ... You chewed the dust that was once a solidly built city, you chewed a bit of Friedrichstrasse or the Anhalter Bahnhof,

for the wind was the only thing that could move freely in Berlin."

Nevertheless it seemed as though a way would be found that could lead out of the agony without conflict. On 17 May 1945 the Soviet occupying force established a democratic city government under Dr. Arthur Werner. Hopes were raised for Potsdamer Platz when highly experienced architect Hans Scharoun (1893–1972) became councillor for building and housing. The first fruits of work on Berlin's urban development were published as early as August in an exhibition called "Berlin plant" ("Berlin is making plans"). For Berlin was to remain one, despite the four-power administration that had emerged since the arrival of the occupying forces of the three western allies from 4 July and the start of work on the inter-allied military command on 7 July.

This made Potsdamer Platz into a kind of "three-countries-corner". Here the three districts of Mitte

*Potsdamer Platz, on the
right are the Columbushaus
and remains of Schinkel's
gatehouses.*

Kappelhöfer, March 1946

100

(Soviet sector), Tiergarten (British sector) and Kreuzberg (American sector) were adjacent to each other. And so the square had an opportunity to play its predestined role as a linking element between the parts of Berlin once more. But it did not have the buildings to do this: of the fifty in the immediate area of the square only twelve had survived to the extent that they could be made functional again with a certain amount of time and effort. Gradually a few retailers, cinema owners and all those who wanted to earn a living from business with more than one sector began to establish themselves here.

But the black market was the main beneficiary from this ideal terrain where you could avoid raids in one sector by taking a few steps into two others. The square was soon dominated by types that had not formerly been typical here. A "nimble mixture of pushers, black marketeers, whores and criminals" set the scene. Spectacular actions by city and military police were on the agenda.

The city's joint administration could develop only in dependence on world politics. And here the prospects for Potsdamer Platz were extremely bad. The fundamentally antagonistic ideas of the three Western powers' politicians and of the Soviet Union about international politics after the Second World War led to constant conflict between East and West. The Cold War culminated in the Air Lift, the division of Berlin and the foundation of two independent German states. It now caused political tensions on 12 August 1948 when Soviet military personnel pursued back marketeers a few dozen metres into the American and British sectors in the course of a raid, with the result that force was used and a few shots were fired. The sector boundary in Potsdamer Platz was now marked by barbed wire entanglements and in other places by lines

of luminous paint on the asphalt. This gave a hint of the direction in which events were moving.

Because of the political and administrative division there was no more joint urban development planning. The former centre of Berlin, Potsdamer and Leipziger Platz, had become a merely peripheral phenomenon for local politicians in both parts of the city. Thoughts about it were pushed away, banished into the distant future. But in 1953 it returned to the centre of things. The slow rate of development in the GDR as opposed to West Germany and West Berlin had become more and more visible. When price rises and norm increases were announced in East Berlin the first strikes and a demonstration took place on the building sites of Stalinallee (Karl-Marx-Allee). The people's movement had been political in character from the beginning, as it was partly directed against the administrative practices, clearly increasing on strength, of a Stalinist regime that was becoming ever more firmly established.

On the next day a demonstration procession of thousands of building workers and workers from several large companies was formed. It moved to the House of the Ministries in Leipziger Strasse, and other demonstrators came across Potsdamer Platz to meet it, most of them from West Berlin. Conditions similar to those of civil war had started to develop in many parts of the city, and the movement spread to other places in the GDR. The Columbushaus, the ruin of "Haus Vaterland" and kiosks in Potsdamer Platz went up in flames, shops in Leipziger Strasse were plundered. Then Soviet tanks rolled along Leipziger and Wilhelmstrasse in the direction of Potsdamer Platz and enforced the state of emergency which was proclaimed at 1 p.m.

Page 102: Potsdamer Platz
involved in the events of 17 June
1953. The colossal hulk of the
Columbushaus, half burnt out in
the Second World War, is once
more a victim of the flames.

Zentralbild, 1953

Leipziger Platz and Leipziger
Strasse on 17 June 1953.
Soviet tanks restore "order"
for the SED government,
which had got into difficulties.
The burnt-out Wertheim
building is on the left of
Leipziger Strasse in the background, and on the right is the
former Herrenhaus.

Zentralbild, 1953

The Columbushaus seen from Kemperplatz.

B. Sass, 11. 4. 1956

The Potsdamer Bahnhof.

I. Lommatzsch, c. 1957

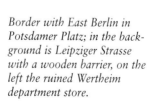

Border with East Berlin in Potsdamer Platz; in the background is Leipziger Strasse with a wooden barrier, on the left the ruined Wertheim department store.

Gert Schütz, 6. 8. 1956

And so Potsdamer Platz had announced its return to the affairs of the city. But it was punished by even greater lack of attention from East and West. It became a part of the peripheral distancing and barrier zone that was dividing the two halves in a way that looked increasingly insurmountable. When after the 13 August 1961 the division of Berlin was literally "cemented" by the building of the Wall, the first reaction on the Eastern side was with pickaxe and bulldozer, under the compulsion of an absolute approach to security. The Columbushaus, the Wertheim ruin, the remains of the new Reichskanzlei and the gatehouses in Leipziger Platz were "tidied away", along with other ruins. A desolate strip of sand and grass up to a hundred metres wide – to give the border guards an unobstructed view and space in which to shoot – ran along the Wall from the Brandenburger Tor to south of Potsdamer Platz, broader than anywhere else. Only the asphalt corner of the roadway in Leipziger Platz and half filled-in, walled-up entrances to the U- and S-Bahn (underground and metropolitan railway) roughly marked the site of the once so famous double square.

Demolition outweighed new building in West Berlin in this area as well. Much fell victim to the pickaxe that could still have been rebuilt or extended: the Anhalter Bahnhof, the Exzelsior and Nürnberger Hof hotels, the Prinz-Albrecht-Palais, the former arts and crafts school and the Völkerkundemuseum (ethnology museum).

But in about 1965 general open development began with a few high- and low-rise buildings around Askanischer Platz. The high point in these efforts was undoubtedly the reconstruction of the Kunstgewerbemuseum (Martin-Gropius-Bau), to 1981. And a few things changed to the west of Potsdamer Platz as well.

Here we find the only building to be rebuilt in its historical form between 1956 and 1960: ·the St. Matthäuskirche. Alongside it works of modern architecture emerged; they triggered heated discussion and gave the area a look that was all its own. The Philharmonie (concert hall), built from 1960 to 1969 to plans by Hans Scharoun, Mies van der Rohe's Neue Nationalgalerie, built from 1965 to 1968, and Hans Scharoun's Staatsbibliothek (state library), 1967 to 1978, have become the core of an area intended to flank Potsdamer Platz as a Kulturforum. It definitely destroyed the historic street pattern once and for all. All thinking ended at the western tangent.

Planning in the East – a general development plan that was continually changed or modified – and the

West – ultimately the 1984 FNP or Land Utilization Plan – suggested nothing for Potsdamer Platz, and design decisions were postponed indefinitely.

First the policy of perestroika in the Soviet Union, then its extension to other Eastern European

Top: Members of the Nationale Volksarmee put up barbed wire barriers in Potsdamer Platz. H. Siegmann, 14. 8. 1961
Bottom: The border with East Berlin in Potsdamer Platz. H. Siegmann, 19. 8. 1961

Barriers in Potsdamer Platz, in the background is the Brandenburger Tor.

Kl. Lehnartz, 14. 2. 1964

countries, the opening of the Hungarian border over night, world changes as a result of the disarmament process – many events and developments of this kind created a situation in which the population of the GDR also finally got rid of the old regime in a series of demonstrations that were all the more effective because they were peaceful. The Wall seemed so densely jointed, so solidly concreted – but overnight it started to fragment, the concrete crumbled away under the fingers of politicians from the old power structures. Something had happened on 9 November 1989 that had for a long time been thought impossible: the border was open and the Wall still at best a symbol, but already almost without a function. And so there it is again: the question about the wrecked centre of Berlin.

Commissions, architects and planners are now working at full speed. The Senate is looking for a joint solution for Potsdamer and Leipziger Platz. Public discussion about future development became a heated debate when the Daimler-Benz concern announced plans for building on 64,000 sq.m. of Potsdamer Platz on their own.

The discussion about developing the central area for the future capital concentrates all questions and arguments that ultimately relate to development throughout the city and the region and will help to decide the appearance of the state as a whole. The result will be a yardstick for the way in which we have handled our twice-broken history.

This double square, which advanced over 250 years from being on the periphery of the royal

residence to being the main square in metropolitan Berlin, which has experienced so many uplifting moments in its existence and so many demeaning ones, which in 1935 still excited the world with its vibrant, multi-faceted life, but also caused it stress and outrage, which then sank into rubble and ashes in a hail of bombs and bullets, whose remains were pushed aside and cleared away in a peace that was again only war, Cold War – this square is still at the centre of our historical responsibility. Once more its opportunity has come.

But will it be used?

*Left: "Deutschstunde" ("German Lesson").
Hans W. Mende, August 1986*

*Right: Souvenir hunters, known as "Wall wood-peckers", in Potsdamer Platz, with the Brandenburger Tor in the background.
Rolf Zöllner, January 1990*

*The Wall started to open up shortly after the Potsdamer Platz crossing point was set up.
Hans W. Mende, November 1989*

*Following double page: 24 sections of a panorama taken from the roof of Wein-haus Huth. The edges of the images overlap to make them more readily intelligible.
Hans W. Mende, April 1981*

The Staatsbibliothek (state
library) from the roof of the
building in Potsdamer
Strasse/corner of Schöneberger
Ufer. In the foreground is the
new Potsdam Bridge, built
1964/65. Immediately adjacent it on the right is the

anchorage for the old
Potsdam Bridge, 1897/98.

Hans W. Mende, 1985

László F. Földenyi On the Border between Past and Future

There was a time when a man could claim as his own as much land as he could walk round in a day, from sunrise to sunset. That was his land. It was measured by his body. His paces marked the border, the sweat of his body drenched the ground and in the air, which lay above him like a bell, he could hear the panting, the quicker and quicker breathing, even years later. The nearer sunset came the faster he had to walk; he had to be back at his starting point before nightfall. If he did not succeed this meant that he had lost the measurement. And thus the right to the soil.

No wonder that his body and the land he had acquired formed a tight unit; if damage was done to the one then the other would feel it too. They were one body and one soul. And the soil that kept the man alive took him in again after his death and embraced him as a grave, like a womb.

Links with our native soil are ancient, and cannot be explained through property; the wish to own land is not one of man's basic needs. Closeness to native soil is also not explained by love of nature; by the time that developed a great deal had damaged the old relationship with the soil. And the need to work and strive for self-sufficiency is also not an explanation; they are more like means

to keep a more profound and more determining wish alive. What is this more profound wish?

It is being at home in a world that is human in its scale, and manageable, that can be peopled by the imagination and whose infinity conveys a feeling of freedom, not helplessness. A cosmic being-at-home, which is not to be understood as the cosmos in a physical sense. The womb offers a cosmic sense of being at home, but so does the grave; harmony with a higher order is unbroken in both cases. And cosmic being-at-home offers a natural relationship with the earth, the soil. It is no co-incidence that the womb is compared with the heavens in many mythologies: it arches like a bell over the earth, which feeds mankind with the life-giving juices.

The earth supports and carries man; when he knows its laws and knows how to handle them he feels at home upon it. And in this case the earth does not simply mean farmland, meadow, pasture or woodland, but much more a projection of the world that is manageable for man; it means that within which he recognizes the secret rhythm of his own life as in a mirror, and which therefore protects him like a shield against the boundlessness of human emptiness. And so the earth's laws are valid

View from the Parey villa of
the Staatsbibliothek, left, the
Neue Nationalgalerie, right,
and the church of St. Matthäus
in the foreground.

Hans W. Mende, 1980

not just "in the open air", in places where no-one dwells, but everywhere man can gain a foothold and establish himself. That is also true in the city. Like men and women who work the land and the fields, city-dwellers have also developed their own laws and customs. They are different of course, but in their way they try to satisfy man's deep wish that has already been mentioned. In the "depths" of the city, in the tangle of its streets and squares the rhythm in which man recognizes the rhythm of his own life will sooner or later be revealed. And if the city can offer him a home, then this rhythm will fill him with profound satisfaction; he can be just as much touched by cosmic being at home amidst the blocks of flats, alleyways, squares and parks as in a deserted landscape, on the edge of a wood, the bank of a river. And while he is looking at the town, strolling through it, walking in it he is at the same time penetrating its body. The invisible map of his life corresponds precisely with the visible map of the city, the life-rhythm of his organism and that of the city are in harmony.

In 1988/89 I spent a year in the western part of Berlin. Most of the time I worked at home. I collected the books that I needed for my work from the Staatsbibliothek. My study was near to the Grunewald, in a short, quiet street, and the books at the other end of this half of the city. I usually went there by car, parking as close to the entrance as possible. For a long time the few steps from the car to the door where my only physical contact with the area around the library.

Later on the number of steps increased. At first, I risked going to the Nationalgalerie opposite, then to the box office of the Philharmonie, and later still even as far as the Kunstgewerbemuseum. I risked it; stepping out of the door of the library I first measured up my destination mentally, and then I turned in the appropriate direction and quickly set off with my head held low, over the wide, six-lane road, only looking ahead or to the side at the most necessary and dangerous moments. I paid attention to my feet and the regular concrete slabs. I had the measure of them, I could relate to them. These slabs were a comfort to me in the gigantic, empty concrete desert. And when I discovered that on every third step I could tread precisely in the centre of a slab they conveyed almost exactly the same feeling of being at home to me as the silent villas of the Grunewald.

I could tread on the paving-stones. They took up the rhythm of my steps and I found a lively relationship with them. Every step conjured a little spark of being at home between the gigantic buildings around and the deserts all about them.

But with every further step I took it was all over with the foot's breadth of home. The desert immediately sucked in the trace of my steps and the buildings pushed me to and fro, instead of guiding

The Kulturforum from the
roof of the building at the corner of Potsdamer Straße and
Schöneberger Ufer. View of
the Neue Nationalgalerie in
the foreground, left in the
background are the Tiergarten
and the Kongreßhalle, in front
of that the Kunstgewerbe-
museum (arts and crafts
museum) and the church of St.
Matthäus, right in the background is the Reichstag, in
front of it the Philharmonie,
the musical instruments museum and the chamber music
hall building site.

Hans W. Mende, 1985

114

and directing me. I was pleased when I could go in somewhere. Not only because that meant I didn't have to suffer from the wind any more, which blew in this strange, formless area even when the rest of the city was completely calm, but also because I was inwardly relieved: as though the infinity was over for a time. It is only a few hundred metres from the Staatsbibliothek to the Philharmonie; even though I was stepping along busily the distance grew into measurelessness.

I have often covered many times this distance in the city centre without noticing. For example, when I went along Pestalozzistrasse, across Bleibtreustrasse and along Niebuhrstrasse, so that I could get to Knesebeckstrasse via Wieland- and Mommsenstrasse, my feet never got tired at all. And that was not only because as a reward, in Savignyplatz, for me probably Berlin's most homely and architecturally perfect square there was a café waiting for me, on whose terrace I could rest, but also because on the way I discovered something new at every step, something I had never seen before.

Walks at the end of Potsdamer Strasse, near the Staatsbibliothek, are quite different. These walks were wearisome and demanding, as if I had to perform the labours of Sisyphus on flat terrain. Perhaps I shouldn't call them walks, but a punishment. In the course of the year I have never met anyone there whose face did not have a scarcely concealed shadow of constraint. All of them gave the impression that they had taken a deep breath and wanted to get out of the area as quickly as possible. They were making an effort, just as I was. Anyone who ends up here feels as though the surrounding air has become more refined; they breathe more rapidly, and walk faster. The surrounding buildings are apparently neutral, but they make even the gait, the body language of people

walking between them into something unnatural. It is clear, it is impossible to go for a walk like that, because if you are out for a walk it is essential to forget yourself. Man gives himself to his surroundings; he entrusts himself to something that at first seems to be outside him, but then becomes a copy of his inner self. A walk – that is trust. But it requires trust not just of your inner self, but also of the "outside" world. And walking, being on one's way then becomes a walk, something that blends the two things together. Street and square become my inner street, my inner square. The walk is also a kind of being at home.

I never had the idea that I could go for a walk in the area around the Staatsbibliothek with my wife or my friends. In the evenings I was particularly struck by the fact that the area was so dead. And when I later learnt that this section of Potsdamer Strasse was not part of the former Potsdamer Strasse, as the library building acts as a barricade across the street's former route, I felt my idea that this is a dead area was confirmed. The six lanes run through a place where there used to be buildings, and on the footpath I am walking through what used to be front gardens, studies, living rooms, bedrooms, shops, cafés, restaurants, and by disturbing the peace of the dead this way I become part of a ghostly world myself. If there is an opposite to the feeling of cosmic being-at-home, this is it.

Viewing platform in Potsdamer Platz, pulled down in late November 1989.

Hans W. Mende, 1981

When I came to Berlin for a long time in the year 1988 I came from an unfixed world: from Hungary, which was about to leave the Eastern bloc without any hope of being able to join the West. The whole country was slightly reminiscent of no man's land, it had a past of its own, and also a vague image of the future, but it seemed to have lost its present.

Then 1989 came along; the situation became more and more chaotic – admittedly, more hopeful as well, as a result. I leafed through the newspapers in the Berlin Staatsbibliothek. The German press was devoting a great deal of attention to Hungary at that time. Of course I felt to a certain extent that the messages and commentaries directed at Hungary were really aimed at the eastern half of Germany, that country whose larger-than-life blocks of flats and never-cleared building sites I could see from the library's second-floor windows.

And because Hungary was increasingly noticeably affected by the fate of the East German refugees, it seemed to me that both countries needed each other much more than in the past decades of official friendship. In this way the Wall became more significant for me; I was also an Eastern European, but my country was now this side of the Wall, and East Germany on the other side. The Wall no longer just divided the East from the West, it also divided the East itself. When I came out of the library and – rarely enough – went "round the back", towards the Wall, I felt confused: I would have had difficulty in saying on which side I was "at home". Because of my past I belonged "over there", but my future called me to "this" side.

And my present? That remained somewhere in the middle, in the Potsdamer Platz area. Somewhere around the library's back exit, intended for lorries, transport workers and staff, the people who have to remain unseen. In Hungary this is called the "service entrance". My present was somewhere there.

When I came back to Berlin for a longer period again, in autumn 1990, I needed the library again. Again I drove there by car, and when the front car-park was full I used the one in Schellingstrasse. Once I forgot to turn off to the right and suddenly there was a huge empty piece of land in front of me. An edge of the town in the middle of the town; a wilderness that was equally reminiscent of a ruined site and a goose meadow; a no man's land in which an unknown war seemed still to be going on. This was Potsdamer Platz, once the city's centre and symbol, familiar from old films, photographs and novels.

As an Eastern European I continued to be certain how I should categorize myself. The deserted,

View of the Wall in Potsdamer Platz.

Hans W. Mende, 1979 (from the "Grenzbegehung" series)

117

desolate quality of the square reflected my situation a little, or more precisely: that of the region from which I came, which was being enlivened by coming to terms with the past and the hope of a truly new future.

The whole of Eastern Europe had the same fate in store for it as this square: they were to be built up again, "used", "worldly" – in brief, enjoyable for people. "Democracy", "freedom", "state founded on the rule of law" and so on: Eastern Europe claimed these concepts for itself for forty years, but the result was a desolation of mind and spirit comparable only with the desolation of Potsdamer Platz. In 1989 the slogans burst like soap bubbles, or people tried to give them a new content. And all that on the basis of a new expectation unambiguously directed at connecting up with the West, which again is to be understood almost exclusively as an economic necessity.

But Potsdamer Platz does not just divide the East from the West, but also the West from the East. Two worlds meet in this square. Or rather, they collide there. The present condition of the square shows that this is a violent, an unnatural encounter. If the contact between the two worlds were natural, the square would not be reminiscent of a wound on the body of the city.

But it is not natural because it cannot be natural. The division of Europe is unnatural in itself. And this unnaturalness has its history and its past. The fate of Eastern Europe was sealed by horse-trading when the United States and the Soviet Union divided Europe up among themselves. This deal and the decline of Potsdamer Platz happened at about the same time: first it was bombed to pieces by the Allies, then the Russians shot the rest of the ruins to bits. First the two worlds became allies, then they stood face to face in the same square with a border marked between them. Both events turned out to be equally fateful for the square. But fate had probably been hanging over the square since the foundation of the German Reich a century ago, when it and the surrounding area gradually became the diplomatic centre and concentrated an enormous variety of power centres around itself to an ever more frightening extent until 1945. The present state of Potsdamer Platz is evidence not just of Allied bombers and Russian artillery, but also of an alarming fatefulness. It is like a stage in the last act of a tragedy of fate.

It seems as though the curtain fell with the Wall. The tragedy is over. Or is there still a satyr play to come? The square – or better, the wilderness to which it belonged – gives a view of the modern blocks of flats in East Berlin and the Kulturforum in West Berlin. The flats give the impression of being ugly and repellent mass-produced items

Shells of buildings in Leipziger Strasse, a Honecker government building project that was stopped after the border was opened and had to make way for the new planning in Leipziger Platz.

Detlev Konnerth, 17. 2. 1990

– houses built for human beings, but in reality silos for human beings, even outwardly bearing the stamp of the kind of reality that is most inimical to human life. And the Kulturforum is a world of ghosts: the library, the Philharmonie and the museum do certainly celebrate Scharoun's and Mies van der Rohe's imagination, but as soon as one steps closer the reality created by this imagination is unmasked as something as oppressive as Albert Speer's vision of flattening the some-time middle-class district and building the a north-south axis for the capital of the Reich.

And all this makes the Eastern European visitor staggering about between the heaps of rubbish in Potsdamer Platz feel somewhat at a loss. He knows the eastern side well; he is sick to death of state dictatorship, and also of other people deciding how he should want to live, in what sort of a flat, in what sort of a building, in what sort of a human silo. He no longer wants others to decide the measure by which he also determines his inner self. But when he looks at the western side he is put in an embarrassing position. This was what he had longed for all the time he was "over there": free imagination, beauty, airy architecture, squares designed organically. What he sees does justice to this completely in terms of detail. But all in all it seems ghostly; he remembers clearly the horror he felt when he had to move from one building to another. And although he knows that he cannot generalize that, the western side of Potsdamer Platz fills him with suspicion.

And what is the cause of this unease? It is that he senses a ghostly symmetry. Here state dictatorship and the dictatorship of planning and technology face each other. Both of them have neglected human beings in their calculations, forgotten them – the passer-by who wants to feel at home in his

city, who before the war was forced out of this district by authorities and institutions and who cannot help the fact that this part of the city was destroyed.

During the war Potsdamer Platz and its surroundings were pulled from under his feet, and when buildings went up in the areas on the two sides of the border – like two distant planets whose orbits never cross – without the one side considering the extent of the other, the city was pulled from over his head as well. Not even if he wanted could he create a home for himself here, "over there" as little as here, let us say between the Philharmonie and the Nationalgalerie, where Theodor Fontane's creations felt so much at home that even a stranger can begin to feel homesick for a place that he has never seen. Technology has won: the spirit of calculation, which decided with ruler and compasses about things that cannot be grasped in that way.

Jumble sale in Potsdamer Platz, left in the background is Weinhaus Huth, and right the Tempodrom.

Hans W. Mende, 1983

After the opening of the Wall and establishment of a border crossing in Potsdamer Platz on 12. 11. 1989.

Hans W. Mende, 13. 11. 1989

But for the time being Potsdamer Platz is still a wilderness. A black hole from which good or bad could emerge: passion, coldness, barbarism, stupidity, madness, genius – or a mixture of all of them. There are buildings on both sides of the empty square; apparently it is only a question of ruler and compasses, and then in a short time the square itself will be built up. And this might easily give an illusion that it depends only on the imagination of the artists competing with each other there how this mixture will be made up.

But the square is also reminiscent of a vacant gaze, that of a person who is having memory problems. And this human look makes one suppose that the real task is not to fill up a neutral, empty square; however striking, ingenious and "full of genius" the technical solution is, perhaps it ought not to become the deciding factor until a later stage. This square is like a sick organism that needs to be talked to kindly, needs human attention and affection before it needs medicine. This square has to bear the burden of a hundred years, of which each of the last fifty weighs many times more than its predecessors. An enormous number of unresolved conflicts has made it what it is: instead of solving them they were continually suppressed with new ones, until finally everything has lost any semblance of a human face.

Leipziger Platz with border crossing.

Detlev Konnerth, 17. 2. 1990

In Potsdamer Platz the passer-by is confronted with the invisible obstacles of history that has become a desert. It is not only his mind and insights that protest, but his body as well. He imagines a future in this square in which the body of the city does not reject him as a foreign body and which he also does not have to pit his own body convulsively against the city's.

If that is to happen this sick part of the city's body must be handled cautiously. This desert cannot be built on from one day to the next; the unsolved historical conflicts cannot be purged with the aid of technology. That would be just the same as stuffing a person who is mentally ill full of medicine and then letting him go. The visitor from Eastern Europe knows from his own experience that future can be created only in places where man has resolved his relationship with the past. And let us add: only then will he have a present as well. If this past is not surveyed and reappraised, then the future too will be a place of death and its décor will be like the new building areas in East Berlin or the Kulturforum's giant hulks. It is about settling up with a world of ghosts, and that also means liberating people from the clutches of a plan that wants to decide about their future instead of them, means resisting the forces that consider everything from industry to environmental protection, but never the incomparable life rhythms of individual human beings – life rhythms which, in the form of concealed or open passion, seek to confront measurelessness with their own measure.

Death and the world of ghosts are always monotonous and homogeneous; life never is. And cosmic feeling-at-home is even less so. If a person develops a feeling for it he will find out that the world in all its multiplicity of colours is his world: it does not confront him like a hostile block, but allows anyone who penetrates it to pass freely through it, to discover and reconnoitre it, to make it his own and then live happily with it. As I always felt happy – I must come back to this again – when I was walking through the area around Savignyplatz, just as I have in squares in any number of other cities that took me in for a while and then sent me on my travels again with a feeling of being at home.

Pedlars by the Wall in Potsdamer Platz, selling fragments of the Wall and caps from the GDR and Soviet armies.
Sabine Sauer, 9. 3. 1990

What is the secret of these squares? We cannot get to the bottom of it simply in terms of architecture, and it cannot be fathomed sociologically either, and town planning elements give just as little information. Every city has a secret that cannot be revealed. If it could be found out then cities could be manufactured in series, something that many people try to do today – and not just cities, places that are called squares as well could be made on conveyor belts. Perhaps the city is a specific variant of the secret of existence? All cities are different from each other, and each has a different secret.

But could it be that every city embodies the same big secret, from Echnaton's El Amarna to the Berlin of the nineties? Is it conceivable that each carries the same insoluble, one secret within it like everything else, like a war, a love, a life path, the history of a philosophical thesis, a longing, a hope, a fear?

This secret can be suppressed, but not fathomed, and even less can it be planned. The secret of a city, a square develops only in the natural course of life; but that life is always that of an organism. Just as – to judge from old photographs – the former Potsdamer Platz was an organism. It is not certain that it was beautiful, and also not certain that it was perfectly planned; but it is certain that it lived, breathed, sighed, suffered, pulsated and perhaps became more and more feverish under threat. The more closely I study the old photographs, and the longer I take over it, the more I am at a loss: I feel that this square too had its secret rhythm. What its secret was I do not know. And I am not sure that I could ever fathom it.

But one thing I do know: I would love to live with this secret. Perhaps then I would have less difficulty with the secret of my own life. If this rhythm were to remain damaged then I would be left to myself in this area, rather like the way in which I felt repulsed when I stepped out of the Staatsbibliothek. I look around and see that I can expect nothing in the immediate vicinity. If I give myself to this place the desert would eat me up from the inside as well. These buildings are very beautiful, and yet it is as though they are trying to block my view of freedom. No wonder that I now prefer looking at the empty Potsdamer Platz site from the library. I still have the possibility of populating it, introducing some variety into it and making it colourful and designing it in such a way that I might possibly be homesick for it some time.

Potsdamer/Leipziger Platz.

Detlev Konnerth, 17. 2. 1990

The oldest building in Potsdamer Platz, which housed the
Ring'sche chemist's shop, shortly
before it was pulled down. Café
Josty, which had previously

become famous in the city centre, moved into the right-hand
new building behind it when it
had to make way for the reconstruction of Schloßplatz.

Friedrich Ferdinand Albert
Schwartz, 1879

Ulrich Pfeiffer

Berlin about to Boom? (and Postscript)

Because of its special history, both parts of Berlin in the past developed very markedly into a city of public service. In East Berlin, centralism produced a concentration of public servants. In West Berlin it was the result of a welfare policy conducted by a state that wanted to secure jobs and prevent migration. Consequently there are now more Federal civil servants working in West Berlin than in Bonn. Hitherto in East Berlin about 32 % of employees worked in the state sector, including political parties. In West Berlin the figure is 235,000, or 25 %. Service provision in the commercial and industrial sector is weakly developed in both parts of the city. Only 44 % and 25 % respectively of employees in commerce and industry worked in the private or commercial and industrial service sector. In contrast, in Hamburg the figure is 61% and in Munich 45%. The explanation for this is simple: in East Berlin, as in the GDR as a whole, services could not develop because the centrally planned economic system simply did not see any need for them, but also proved itself incapable of controlling this complex sector adequately. Tourism and financial services, just like advertising and business consultancy, marketing or auditing eked out a miserable existence. The catching-up growth that the East German Länder will experience in the next few years will concentrate on the service sector to a large extent. This is true at least as far as employment is concerned. Certainly reindustrialization will be needed in parallel with the industrial collapse.

This statement is also true for West Berlin in a different form, as its economy is considerably underdeveloped in terms of comparable West German cities. West Berlin is certainly a major city – Kurfürstendamm, Philharmonie, KaDeWe, Memorial Church, culture and night-life, subcultures and a broad political spectrum, indeed even the riots are signs of a metropolis full of stimuli and tensions. But Berlin also remained a provincial town. Despite a metropolitan cultural life, historical memories, magnificent façades and shopping streets, West Berlin remained a village with millions of inhabitants and an economic structure that is more like Landshut than London, more like Trier than Tokyo.

Measured in employment terms, Berlin is Germany's largest industrial city, but without the high density of research and development of Munich or Stuttgart. Berlin has no combine heads like

*View from the Staatsbiblio-
thek along the old, tree-lined
Potsdamer Strasse to the
Potsdamer/Leipziger Platz
area.*

Sabine Sauer, 9. 5. 1990

126

Hamburg or Düsseldorf. 350 associations have their headquarters in Cologne, in Berlin it is not even worth starting to count. In Frankfurt there are 86 bank and insurance employees per 1,000 inhabitants, in Hamburg the figure is still 34, but 13 in West Berlin. Hamburg is smaller (500,000 fewer inhabitants than West Berlin) but has 80,000 more office workers. At the same time there is less retail sales area in West Berlin (Hamburg 3.3 sq m per inhabitant; Berlin 2 sq m per inhabitant), fewer cars, fewer lawyers, advertising agencies or other high-grade service professions than in other large cities.

There is a simple explanation for West Berlin's backwardness in terms of economic development. Behind the Wall, in an island situation, it was just impossible for high-grade central services to evolve. Lawyers' chambers, brokers, investment companies, large financial concerns, auditing companies, combine heads or highly sophisticated retailing need a hinterland and zones of influence. Tight boundaries have also set boundaries for the economic development of Berlin.

The state has certainly compensated for this where compensation was possible. It moved research institutions and central departments, for example the Federal Environment Office and the Monopolies and Mergers Commission, courts or the Federal Insurance Institute to Berlin. But that is no substitute for a high-grade private service sector.

Berlin's special development, which occurred because of the bulkhead effect of the Wall, is now coming to an end. Berlin's reincarnation as an economic metropolis is beginning. It is not possible to form a clear idea of what this means at the moment. Above all, nobody knows how quickly radical change will come. One might almost wish

for things to go slowly. But that cannot be relied on. Berlin's location potential is considerable:

a) About 4.2 million people live in the Berlin region, the S-Bahn (city railway) and ring motorway systems' catchment area. They and the local economy need services – from shopping facilities to repair shops for cars and televisions, from legal advice via solicitors to advertising and auditing. Above all economic development needs an effective building trade. This is more true for the extension and development trade than for the new building side. Given the low starting level, basic provision of effective services for the local economy and the populace will be an important source of growth.

b) At the same time Berlin will take over important functions for East Germany. Here the own-weight of the local population and economy will develop its own powers of attraction to sites for central service provision. As a large conurbation in the centre of East Germany, as a motorway and rail junction and site of important airports it provides good starting points for the development of a high-grade tertiary sector. In future there will certainly be a high-speed train from Paris via Berlin to Warsaw and Moscow. As well as this, the West Berlin administration is better tuned to our legal system than other cities in the area of the former GDR. It is used to dealing with Western investors. The whole of Berlin will benefit from this. For this reason Berlin will draw service functions to itself that were previously missing like a magnet now the boundaries are down. These include central production-related services in particular (enterprise consultancy, auditing, transport logistics, airlines, wholesalers). But also the whole computer trade, which senses a huge underdeveloped market "on the doorstep" in the East will be intending to develop new markets from Berlin, along with other high-tech providers.

c) It must certainly not be overlooked that many central functions for the Federal Republic as a whole are already divided. Of the 500 largest companies 11 have their headquarters in Berlin, but 53 in Hamburg, 38 in Munich and Frankfurt and 34 each in Düsseldorf and Stuttgart. Despite its size, Berlin's location meant that it was not attractive enough. Company head offices are known for their great site loyalty. Shifts of location by combines will remain the exception in future. Daimler-Benz-AG's decision to move its firm's service organization headquarters to Berlin is itself already an exception. Central high-grade service functions are immobile in broad areas.

Thus Frankfurt will retain its position as Germany's international finance and banking centre. Munich, Hamburg and Frankfurt again retain their role as important insurance centres. However, market shares are not fixed for central functions. New area work divisions will develop in Europe because of the break-up of the Eastern bloc and the EU's shift to the single market. Great Britain, for example, will become a major car exporter again thanks to the arrival of large Japanese motor companies. Eastern European production locations will take over important delivery and complementary functions vis-à-vis Western Europe. Their one-sided orientation to the East will no longer apply. Large concerns will spread their production networks over a larger area. This will lead to a high degree of specialization.

Thus in the sphere of motor industry supplies two or three large companies will service the whole of Europe in sections. As a consequence of the end of the baby boom the search for qualified reserve work forces will lead to direct investment and co-operation with Eastern Europe. The new trade and delivery streams and new area work division and closer co-operation in the production sector will require complementary service functions. That means: new central services are emerging, and they will be looking for new locations. Berlin is very well placed here because of its location.

The decision to move high-grade central services to Berlin or to establish national and international service functions will always be subject to competition between various places. Here potential local demand has a smaller part to play. North German areas are as accessible from Hamburg as they are from Berlin. Enterprise consultants can travel from Munich to Gera as they can from Berlin to Gera. A favourable situation and good conditions are not the sole factors affecting the result of this competition. High-grade services need leisure and cultural facilities, but also high-grade labour and housing markets, an efficient transport system and an attractive educational sector. An efficient administration has to signal and demonstrate how it will influence the city's development in such a way that there are good site conditions for businesses and residents. Services process information. Their raw materials include contacts and relationships. Central service functions go to places where they will find partners, but also competitors or clients. Just as certain streets in major cities have concentrations of jewel-

Potsdamer Platz S-Bahn station.

Robert Paris, 1990

lers' shops, which makes it easier for suppliers and customers to form a clear impression of the market and conduct their business, special concentrations also occur in large cities. Hamburg has wholesale concentrations, Düsseldorf a "Japanese" colony, and Munich a concentration in the software sphere, for example.

Profiles of this kind have yet to emerge in Berlin. Thus it is still not certain whether Berlin can greatly improve its significance as a publishing and media city, after Hamburg has greatly strengthened its position in this sphere in the past. The special cultural traditions of East Germany will certainly produce a corresponding cultural economic sector. That is to say: there are linking and starting points for the development of a high-grade service sector. Pioneering decisions by large companies are important here, as they are the first to make new profiles visible. They produce "bandwagon effects". Large companies or branches of firms work as magnets for others. Magnet and linking effects ahead of or behind an operation, or in related areas, are almost as significant as wealth creation and employment chains in individual large establishments.

Service cities need more charisma, images and symbols than production cities. They need a special climate that their design and architecture also help to shape. They need contact networks. It is harder to create suitable locations for service businesses than for industry. Architecture and political culture are just as important as attractive congresses and concerts. It is too early to prophesy future development paths for the tertiary sector in Berlin scientifically. There is far too much that is still open. But even today one can predict: Berlin's rise as a service metropolis will be different from Hamburg's or Frankfurt's. For example, Berlin cannot say goodbye to its past as a production city. With-out further development of the production base the development of the production-oriented service sector will be hindered. Berlin has to concentrate on service spheres with high growth rates, because the classical central functions have long been divided up between the competitors.

In East Berlin, the high-grade service sector will take off more slowly because outdated organizations will shrink and collapse. This will release offices and workers. At the same time the majority of the old industries in East Berlin and the surrounding area will collapse. Old production sites will shrink or be closed down. But at 25 %, industrial employment in East Berlin remained well behind the 40–50 % achieved in the southern cities of the former GDR, such as Gera, Halle or Chemnitz. But many central planning bureaucracies will become superfluous. The combines have been split up. The security apparatus is dwindling. The bloc parties have already dismantled their staffs. A total of over 150,000 people have lost their office jobs, thus releasing about 2 million sq m of office space. But set against the medium-term growth potential all these releases and collapses are minor.

Berlin, Germany's largest city will also grow faster than any other city, and autonomous economic growth can be further stimulated by new capital city functions, by new government officials, lobbyists, journalists, group bureaucrats and diplomats. It is almost impossible to estimate how many new inhabitants there will be. Barcelona, Lisbon and Madrid have recently shown the kind of growth rates that can be anticipated when catching up on the past.

Potsdamer Platz S-Bahn station.

Robert Paris, 1990

At the same time one can study there what it means to handle this kind of growth. In Madrid office rents are considerably higher than in Frankfurt at present; it has become the third dearest office city in Europe after London and Paris. For Berlin an increase of this kind would mean that in perhaps 15 years it will have an additional city the size of Nuremberg.

This is more than any other city has had to handle since the war in terms of rebuilding. Munich before the Olympic Games was at best a premonition of Berlin as a future building site. The dimensions are more like those of the London City's 80s building record.

Against this thesis, reference is made to the dismantling of state employment in East Berlin, and shrinking industrial employment, especially in the surrounding area. Of course these developments are bound to affect the private service sector. Here there are links. Lack of purchasing power is bound to affect areas like retail or housing demand. But more careful distinctions have to be made here. In industry in the surrounding area and in East Berlin it is not just the number of employees in manufacturing that is being reduced; administrative functions in particular are being dismantled as well, like for example the inspectors and planning bureaucrats needed inside the firms for a centralist planning system.

At the same time the social facilities established in the combines (kindergartens, health provision) have been reduced to practically nothing. But such administrative and social services are re-emerging at least partially in other forms. In a market economy marketing or controlling departments have to be set up. New production-oriented services are coming into being, in part as a mirror image of the former decline. In many cases combine kindergarten workers have simply switched to local authority service, although local authorities today often do not have adequate financial resources. There is considerable transitional friction.

A distinction has to be made between this structural change as a result of a change in system and growth effects in local supply services from commerce to trade or lawyers and tax consultants. East Berlin, judged by Western standards, lacks about 800,000 to 1 million sq m of retail space. There is a lack of bank branches, insurance facilities, squash courts and petrol stations, and above all, after the wave of used car purchases, of car repair shops. A need to catch up is also produced under unfavourable economic development. And yet in future East Germany will have the same experience that we have had in the Western regions. The service sector cannot develop independently of the production sector. High-level industrial growth produces income for consumers and demand for production services and forms the basis for a strong state sector. Conversely, high-grade production services have a favourable influence on industrial competitiveness and thus the overall development of the region.

Therefore the success of re-industrialization and modernization of industry in East Germany is a prerequisite of strong growth in the service sector. Re-industrialization takes longer than planning shopping centres or stations. But it is slowly getting under way. However, it is still impossible to predict whether industrial growth will have caught up completely in five or ten years. Considerable delays will in any case mean a transitional emigration

Potsdamer Platz S-Bahn
station.

Robert Paris, 1990

133

phase. Removing unemployment by emigration could be more significant for some time than removing unemployment by job creation. The range of possible development paths is still very broad from our present viewpoint.

But it is true that there will inevitably be immigration into Berlin as a side effect of growth in the service sector. If employment in banks doubles in 10–15 years, then it will probably be impossible to recruit the top positions in particular from the local labour market alone. Something similar is true of other service areas. An increase of 30,000 people per year in the region from home and abroad, but also from the agricultural areas of Mecklenburg, is entirely possible. This leads to a persisting bottleneck in the housing sector. Rising building and land costs increase rents. The housing shortage will be on a far greater scale than anything we saw in Frankfurt and Munich. Present building activity is by no means adequate to deal with the future leap in demand. 6,000 to 8,000 residential units per year were completed in West Berlin in the 80s. In East Berlin it was 20,000 to 25,000, but in a form that will not be acceptable to the building industry in future. Also the former state finance system for housing construction has collapsed with the transition to monetary and economic union. New sources of finance and investment have to be found alongside a differently structured building economy, as the old combines are no longer there to invest. The new Senate has set a target of completing housing units at a rate of 20,000 per year. This figure is determined more by restricted financial resources than by demand: 30,000 to 40,000 units per year should be financed. The programme is too meagre to meet growing demand. It is in the lap of the gods who will build and finance 30,000 to 50,000 units per year in future. This means that the housing shortage will lead to estates of shacks for building workers who immigrate from abroad or from rural areas. Landlords with an eye for business will rent housing by the room to single people at high prices. Over-occupation and housing queues are becoming a permanent problem. However, there is also the hope that after a certain delay freely financed housing construction will rise in future. Berlin as a tenant city will be able to produce a large number of owner-occupiers in future. There is enough room for large quantities of detached housing in surrounding area.

Potsdamer Platz S-Bahn station.

Robert Paris, 1990

There will be resistance to and protest against this second period of rapid growth in Berlin, parallel with the late 19th century Gründerzeit. The population, revelling today in the demands made on Berlin as capital and metropolis, will come to curse its future new citizens, who will make restaurants and housing dearer, block up the roads and fill the theatres. But effectively Berlin's growth is happening from the outside. Berlin can do nothing but accept this growth, and must design buildings for it, and secure it socially, because without the development of Berlin the former GDR will not make proper progress. Innovation must shine out from here to the whole of Eastern Germany. Berlin will become brain controlling the economic integration of East Germany. Of course Frankfurt and Munich will also provide planning and control decisions through direct co-operation. For Frankfurt this means development of the East German banking sector in particular. And of course concepts for the renewal of East German production plant will also come from Dortmund or Munich. But in the course of time more and more planning and control functions will be concentrated in Berlin.

Faced with the masses of buildings looking for land in Berlin, one can react only with shock, as 80s urban development was scarcely exhilarating where building on large areas was concerned. There are many attractive, often controversial, individual buildings. But in places where coherent parts of the city or whole new estates were developed, what usually emerged was an architectural cackle, a multitude of materials, forms of expression and design variants that tend to bewilder. Subjectivity, or stringing together buildings that elicit an "aha" response, even if they are by good architects, does not add up to urban development.

And yet investors and building financiers are queuing up in Berlin. Office rents in Berlin will explode upwards to 60, 80, 100 marks per square metre and climb as if in an auction. Development pressure is increasing. Politicians are facing a demand to create safety-valves as quickly as possible. At the same time the core city is under pressure of competition from surrounding communities governed by the interests of Brandenburg. The extensive S-Bahn system makes it possible to build industrial parks, shopping centres and office cities outside Berlin. Large insurance companies have for a long time now not been looking for premises in the centre but prefer peripheral sites with good access.

The city can already not meet demands on its infrastructure, large parts of which are ready for the scrap-heap in East Berlin. The streets will be blocked by a million additional cars in the next 10 to 15 years. But it is not possible, as it has been in Frankfurt and Munich, with their concentrated city centres, to carry out large-scale traffic calming measures, because the distances involved are greater in Berlin. It is only by linking traffic planning and building investment that complete overloading in the city centre can be prevented. Without clear guidelines investors will want to develop every open space from the centre outwards as soon as possible. As in other rapidly growing cities, it will be only a few years before the problem arises of having to move new and important functions to unfavourable sites because important areas have been previously occupied.

Potsdamer Platz S-Bahn station.

Robert Paris, 1990

There are two central themes for urban development in Berlin: The basic structure for future spatial development has to be fixed. Here radial development is favoured, following the old stellar S-Bahn network, which reaches far out into the surrounding area. This concept is unavoidable. But any stellar form developing outwards tends to overload the centre. Munich and Paris offer examples of such overloaded centres that are best reached from all points of the compass.

For visitors in the last 20 years Berlin was above all Charlottenburg with its dense metropolitan development, completed since the war. There is no other German city in which – as in the Kurfürstendamm area – there is such a mixture in such a restricted space of old residential buildings with new offices, commercial uses, shops, discotheques, bars and restaurants. This mixture offers a model and an ideal for the inner city areas that are to be redeveloped. But we must not run away with the idea that such a mixture can be reproduced at will. It depends on specific prerequisites. If development pressure and demand are too high then traders looking for a rapid and massive turnover with standard articles drive out high-grade, attractive retail businesses, you will look in vain for antique shops in the side streets. If there is not enough office space, changes of use go on the increase. Overloading would be deadly.

To take the strain off central Berlin, the ring along the city motorway and the S-Bahn could be a key part of its development. Room could be found along this ring for large-scale administrative buildings, insurance buildings, retail centres, for example, but also for mass welfare state administration units which may well be set up in Berlin. It is unlikely that ring development can proceed satisfactorily without powerful controls imposed by urban planning and public institutions, which could set a good example by moving their offices to the ring. Private investors are forcing their way into the centre with all the strength they can muster, even when this will lead to considerable overloading. Room has to be found in the city centre for the inevitable banks and some large administrative centres, who always want to be there, but also above all for retail, important prestigious buildings, hotels, restaurants, cinemas, bars and the expanding service professions. Brokers, lawyers, solicitors, doctors, advertising agencies, auditing companies, financial advisors, property administrators, media agents, travel agents, airline offices and similar customer-intensive uses that bring people into the city and keep them moving need space alongside dense residential areas, which can remain as part of the inner-city mix.

Of course ideas of this kind should not be implemented with a kind of stubborn purism. A centre as large as Berlin can take some large administrative centres. Also a tight market and restricted availability will themselves impose an element of selection. If rents rise to 60 to 80 marks then the tenants will have to earn 8–12,000 marks per month to service rents at this level. Central Berlin will be too expensive for simple administrative centres for the mass data-processing from insurance companies' loss adjustment to the shovelling around involved in clearing cheques. There is nothing for them in the high price zones. They need peripheral sites with good public transport.

*Potsdamer Platz S-Bahn
station.*

Robert Paris, 1990

Independently of the quantitative problems and the problems of growth management of the phasing of investment and planning projects, the content of Berlin's urban development problems is more difficult than elsewhere. You have only to walk from the Reichstag along the Wall strip across Potsdamer Platz to the Gropius building, across the site of the former Gestapo headquarters along Kochstrasse to the Springer skyscraper to recognize how thrown together and worn out some of Berlin's central districts are because of war damage, but also because of planning and building in the past 40 years. Amputated streets side by side with the remains of old buildings (ruined Anhalter Bahnhof), new socialist housing on dead boulevards (Leipziger Strasse), alongside the urban use, already dense, in Friedrichstrasse, new, more open residential building in south Friedrichstadt, the emptiness of the Kulturforum and the green band of the Landwehrkanal represent a challenge for architects and planners of a kind that is more attractive, but also more difficult and requiring a more responsible approach than in any other Western metropolis. And of course this is not just about building forms and design. It is also about fixing the detail of future uses precisely. This will be difficult to achieve politically, as there is no context to force decisions into being. The available areas are too large and too undefined. Future urban structure and use patterns would have to be thought out ahead in scenarios. This means for example that the building masses and land needs that now have to be redistributed have to be assessed. Does Berlin-Mitte need 1 million or 1.5 million sq m of retail space? How much of the 3 to 4 million sq m of office space that will probably be built in the next 15 years can be sited in Berlin-Mitte? How much will have to be accommodated on the ring and how much on peripheral sites?

The most important location conditions are now being created by fixing the public local transport system. Intensive retail zones requiring high user-frequency and thus a high demand on good local public transport will form in future at S-Bahn and U-Bahn junctions and along the important axes. Specialist and luxury shops will come into being in side and neighbouring streets off the main axes of retail concentration. In between these offices that have less need for sites with intensive public transport will find their place. Given the large areas that have hitherto been undefined Berlin, unlike other large cities, is not able to move forward in small steps. A basic structure will have to be established by political discussion. Here of course it does not make any sense to plan new shopping streets or zones in several places at the same time, for example, without knowing what purchasing power is there to be distributed or what pedestrian densities are to be expected. It makes no sense to plan office concentrations or encouraging ideas of mixed use without knowing the price and rent levels that will be reached.

At present the magic words "urban development ideas competition" are frequently to be heard. Such competitions have to exist, but it cannot be left to architects who have flown in from New York, London or Milan, however good they are, to fix the future structure of the city. And it can just as little be local architects' responsibility to determine the structure of Berlin as a metropolis. Neither can investors be given a free hand to fix building density and use according to their individual economic profitability calculations. Politicians have to make the fundamental decisions. They have to devise an urban structure in a dialogue with urban developers and other experts and thus set down requirements so that investors, who plan and make decisions independently, will know the context into which they are building. Of course such decisions do not express free political evaluations. One cannot decree pedestrian areas if the distances to be walked are too great or if there is too little happening along the pavements. One cannot prescribe a mixture of offices and shops if the rents that can be charged for the shops will not cover the building costs. Housing can be built on high-grade sites, but with the consequence that possible uses there that create intensive customer and commercial contact will come about elsewhere and thus overload the transport sector.

A comparison of Frankfurt and Munich shows the range of possible choices. In Frankfurt the decision went in favour of a high concentration of jobs in high-rise, inner-city offices. In Munich, which has an office market of roughly the same size and comparable office building activity, the decision was taken to permit high-rise building on the middle ring only. Investment was shifted outwards at an earlier stage and spread over a greater area. This means that the whole city area inside the middle ring has remained a mixture of housing, offices and shops. But it is true that an increasing number of overloading phenomena are becoming visible in the actual core city because of the stellar form of the local transport system. Berlin has the opportunity to learn from urban development experience in Frankfurt and Munich, London and Madrid. The wealth of material and insights than can be acquired from these examples should be sufficient to make decisions about structure in an informed and competent manner. It is only on the basis of such decisions that architects can set about their work successfully.

And there is also the great anxiety that the multiplicity of expressive forms, materials and subjective "languages" that characterize contemporary archi-

tecture will have a chaotic, restless and hectic effect if applied en masse to central Berlin. Given the inclination to present an architecture of eclectic quotations everywhere, for Berlin one would wish for greater calm, simple, manageable urban figures that are easy to grasp. Given the profits that the investors can expect, and given the building volumes awaiting architects, there will be no lack of investment capital or talent. Entrepreneurs and building financiers, workers and managers, brokers and project developers will stream to Berlin from all over the place. The bottleneck will be not talent, sources of finance and forms of organization, but an ability to tame all this, to focus it and pour it into a mould that will allow us to recognize Berlin in 20 years time. Berlin in 2010 must not look like the "parrot architecture" of Docklands or the accumulation of towers in New York's Madison Avenue. Even in 15 years one would like to be able to say, despite perhaps another 4 million sq m of offices, despite 400,000 additional dwellings: "Berlin is still Berlin".

Postscript

After I wrote my essay "Berlin About to Boom?" in spring 1990 Germany went into recession after the reunification boom, but this recession is now over. This means that the considerable economic changes about which only expectations could be expressed in 1990 have now come about. Here it has become clear that the anticipated de-industrialization in the Berlin/Brandenburg region has taken on some of the features of a crisis. At the same time the expansion of the service sector has clearly slowed down. It will only get under way again at the end of the decade, when the government makes its (delayed) move to Berlin.

This slow-down in demand is set against a completion boom in the office sector that will lead to an enormous supply excess in 1996/97. The extension of special write-offs for property investment, in place until 1997, triggered a final completion spurt that will last for a long time. The supply excess combined with the expiry of the tax concession will cause an abrupt interruption of production. At present it is impossible to say how long it will take for demand to absorb the excess, bringing about the possibility of increased office building activity again.

Housing construction has also seen a similar development. The exorbitant tax concessions for investors (50 % special write-off) have triggered an unprecedented building boom, complemented by large housing construction programmes in Berlin. In the surrounding area it was the generous designation of building land that led to low building land prices, a substantial prerequisite for a major increase in building activity. Overall, after the completion of 20,000 dwellings in 1994, about another 65,000 dwellings are bound to have been completed in 1995 and 1996. This means that the housing market bottlenecks of 1990 to 1994 have been dealt with for the time being. But certainly high investment activity in the surrounding area in particular will come to a standstill for a long time. Freely financed building of rented dwelling will become profitable again only after many years of high rent increases, on the basis of worse tax conditions. The great variations in building activity, above all the tax recession arising as a consequence of the expiry of special write-offs from 1997, will contribute to the persisting instability of economic development in Berlin, which continues to be characterized by rapid rebuilding and a considerable sectoral structure-change. Expansion has so far been very one-sided. High growth in the building sector and expanded employment in the tertiary sector were set against a dramatic collapse in industrial employment. The build-up of new, competitive high-tech industries will still need some time here, and move forward only gradually. Rising employment in the "capital city sector" will also be weaker than anticipated in the early 90s.

The city of Berlin will scarcely be recognizable after nineties building activity in Berlin-Mitte and parts of the Tiergarten, Charlottenburg, Kreuzberg and Friedrichshain districts. And in the surrounding area increasing suburbanization can be seen. In the 1992 to 1995 phase more major urban development programmes were started in Berlin than in Munich, Frankfurt and Hamburg put together. A new Gründerzeit is happening in central Berlin as far as urban development is concerned. This building activity will be one of Berlin's chief characteristics for a long time to come.

View north-west across the former Potsdamer Bahnhof site. On the right is Weinhaus Huth in Linkstrasse, which *runs diagonally across the picture.*

Robert Paris, October 1990

143

*Neue Reichskanzlei, garden
façade on Voßstrasse.
Former Reichskanzlei gar-
den with remains of the
"Führerbunker".*

*Wolfgang Gehrke,
May/June 1949*

Alfred Kernd'l

From Baroque to Bunker

Berlin is the capital again, and is to be the seat of Germany's government. Whether the Berliners, and above all the politicians responsible, are up to the task will also be measured against the extent to which the city can perceive and prove itself to be credible as a historically aware metropolis, over and above the desire for security of its economy and jobs – for example in its future handling of the force field that is Potsdamer or better Leipziger Platz, with its quarter of a millennium of bursting with history, which will be mentioned only in terms of its highlights.

Two hundred and fifty years ago and for a long time after that there was no Potsdamer Platz, but a Potsdamer Tor: a gateway to complete the Octogon created by Frederick the Great's father. This original gateway situation was later replaced by a square in name only. Schinkel suggested a design involving peripheral planting with trees, but this was short-lived, and failed mainly because of increasing traffic, even in the 19th century, concentrated here from five directions. Baedeker's late 19th and early 20th century guides characteristically mentioned only the enormous amount of traffic in this "less than extensive" square (be careful when crossing) and preferred to expatiate on Leipziger Platz, the Octogon's new name after the Wars of Liberation.

This essay will deal with the historic site north of Leipziger Platz, bordered to the east by the former Wilhelmstrasse, to the west by the Wall, until a few months ago and to the north by the Brandenburger Tor and Pariser Platz (originally Quarré, but renamed after the Wars of Liberation, like the Octogon). These boundaries had been set since the baroque period in which they originated. Nicolai formulated them succinctly in his late 18th century description of Berlin: "the gardens of all the above-mentioned palaces in Wilhelmstrasse, on the left, up to the city wall, between the octagon and the square". Nicolai's city wall was the excise wall built by the Soldier King, which was also intended to prevent desertion by the pressed men of the Berlin garrison. It was pulled down in the middle of the previous century, but re-emerged on this site almost precisely to the metre as the Wall belonging to the most recent past.

The area was opened up and developed when Friedrichstadt was extended west from Mauerstrasse by Friedrich Wilhelm I. The basic structure of palaces for the nobility with long pleasure gardens behind them did not disappear until after the Second World War. The historic topography of the place where important ministries had been established in the 19th century, and where

Entrance to the bunker area.
Maria Ulrich, 8. 6. 1990

West wall of the bunker
with frescos.
Height of frescos c. 1 metre

the Reichskanzlei had been since 1875 and the Reich President's palace from 1918, had been extinguished. Some of the bunkers that were part of the Reichskanzlei were not included in the clearance.

In 1875 the German Reich had the former Schulenburg palace at 77 Wilhelmstrasse converted as an official residence for the Reich's Chancellor. The palace had been dedicated in 1739, in the presence of Friedrich Wilhelm I. Its first owner was Graf Adolf Friedrich Schulenburg, a critical friend of Crown Prince Friedrich since their time in Küstrin, who was ungraciously treated by the young king ("I saw a Schulenburg squadron that was confusion itself"). The cavalry commander had to experience the unfortunate action by the Prussian cavalry at the battle of Mollwitz on 10 April 1741 before he fell.

Later Friedrich's brothers Ferdinand and Heinrich lived here, Gräfin Dönhoff, mistress to Friedrich Wilhelm II, and Fürst Radziwill. Bismarck resided here from 1875 until his dismissal in March 1890 ("We were put out in the street like thieves"). Bismarck led the Congress of Berlin as an "honest broker" in the Reichskanzlerpalais from 13 June to 3 July 1878. Finally Hitler extended his official residence along Voßstrasse in the form of Speer's Neue Reichskanzlei building on the site of 78 Wilhelmstrasse, previously occupied by the Marschall palace.

This palace, built in 1736 by Gerlach for Minister of State von Marschall, originally had the largest garden in the area. Achim and Bettina von Arnim had their first home after they were married in the garden house here, and Bettina wrote to Goethe: "I live here in paradise. The nightingales sing lustily in the chestnut trees outside my bedroom window, and the moon, which has never shone so brightly, wakes me with its full beams."

The palace was pulled down in the 1870s, when Voßstrasse was being realigned. It was incidentally no coincidence that this street, named after the last owner of the estate, ran along an old parcel boundary of the Marschall garden, as can be seen by comparing the current street map with Schmettau's plan, an example of the long term historical effect of even a partial plot boundary.

When the Neue Reichskanzlei was built in the former Marschall garden, work started on a bunker system that was completed only in the Second World War. Parts of this underground command headquarters have survived until today, because they are so robust, and so deep under the ground. They are the only compact and authentic evidence of the history of this place to have survived in situ. The parts of the Alte and Neue Reichskanzlei that survived the war were first used by the Soviet victors as a quarry for their monuments. The Germans then finally pulled them down; in both the east and the west they were pleased to get rid of the past when it had turned to stone, often enough with an eagerly sought alibi commission from the victorious powers. The most recent example of this is the demolition of the war criminals' prison in Spandau in 1987.

It is well known that bunkers can be removed only with great difficulty. Over the decades, and it took many attempts, explosions decimated the actual "Führerbunker" of the Reichskanzlei. All that remain of it are the foundation slab and fragments of the concrete outer walls. Intact remains of the bunker system ultimately survived only because they were below the surface, and thus did not cloud the German eye's need for harmony,

South wall of the bunker with frescos.
Height of frescos c. 1 metre
Maria Ulrich, 8. 6. 1990

East wall of the bunker with frescos.
Height of frescos c. 1 metre
Maria Ulrich, 8. 6. 1990

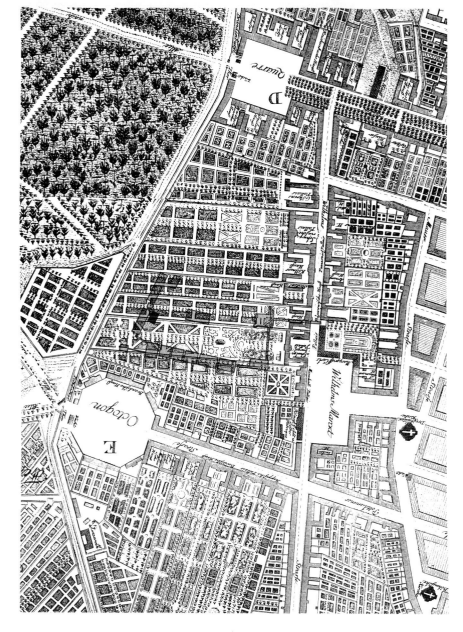

The Reichskanzlei bunker system transposed to scale on to Schmettau's 1748 plan. The "Führerbunker" is in the north-east of the complex. The bunker with the frescos is in the west (red).

According to the most recent investigations, apart from the fresco bunker only a few along Voßstrasse remain. Schmettau's plan, as was often the custom at the time, is oriented south-

north. To make it easier to understand it has been turned north-south here, and is thus standing on its head.

and, paradoxically, in the last three decades because they were protected by the Wall and the death strip.

In March 1990 the past unexpectedly made a brief re-appearance. A provisional entrance to some of the bunkers along Voßstrasse was opened up briefly under a shallow mound in the former death strip, in the context of a warm-hearted united German tree-planting action of all things. A "coming-to-terms" discussion flickered into life that did not bode well for the future. The spectrum of the conservative right tended to be embarrassed, and kept its head down. The liberal-progressive camp was inclined to remove this "absolute non-place", "monstrous legacy", "cabinet of horrors". This tendency was at the most prepared to take closed groups through the Nazi underworld, but later, and only after thorough educational enlightenment, in order to avoid the danger of a "brown place of pilgrimage". There was a high degree of excitement, because there was a mistaken impression among the participants in the discussion that this was the "Führerbunker", in which Hitler and Goebbels had died.

The past got in touch again on 6 June 1990. Some ammunition salvage work was going on as part of the preparations for the media spectacle called "The Wall", due to take place on 21 July in the cleared space south of Pariser Platz. In the course of this work a concrete bunker was discovered under a layer of earth and rubble on the former Reichskanzlei site. It was a single-storey structure with an area of about 10 x 30 m, with several rooms. Rotting bunks, remains of shelves, wine bottles, porcelain crockery as well as ammunition and guns showed what conditions were like in the last few days of the war. Russian forces – evidence of their visit was provided by the fact that a flamethrower had been used – can only have been in the bunker very briefly. It had probably been hastily abandoned before the Red Army arrived. It must have been sealed shortly after the end of the fighting and consigned to oblivion. This explains why the frescos in one of the rooms are in such good condition. They illustrate values that were current and official at the time: SS men protecting German couples and tipplers with shields, eagle symbols, oak leaves and Gothic German-jingoistic initials for "Leibstandarte Adolf Hitler" (Adolf Hitler's personal bodyguard). The manner of execution suggests an amateur artist from the bodyguard, which provided guards and drivers (the latter had been allotted this bunker) for the Reichskanzlei. The scenes of war featuring English soldiers must relate to the Balkan campaign. This means that the paintings date from early summer 1941.

As the bunker was sealed off again after only two days, and it had been possible to keep its opening relatively secret, the find did not cause much of a stir, despite the frescos, at least in Germany. But thanks to the alertness of "The Wall" producer Mick Worwood some English newspaper correspondents were allowed in, and reported in more detail, and Mr. Worwood was photographed in front of one of the frescos. Fortunately this was the only commercial exploitation for the pop concert, which is astonishing in view of Pink Floyd's lines "Sitting in a bunker here behind my wall waiting for the worms to come".

Bismarck was sad and embittered because his successor Caprivi "had the ancient trees in front of the garden side of his, formerly my, home cut down. They were an adornment to the official Reich plots of land in the Residence that can be regenerated only in centuries, and therefore irreplaceable …

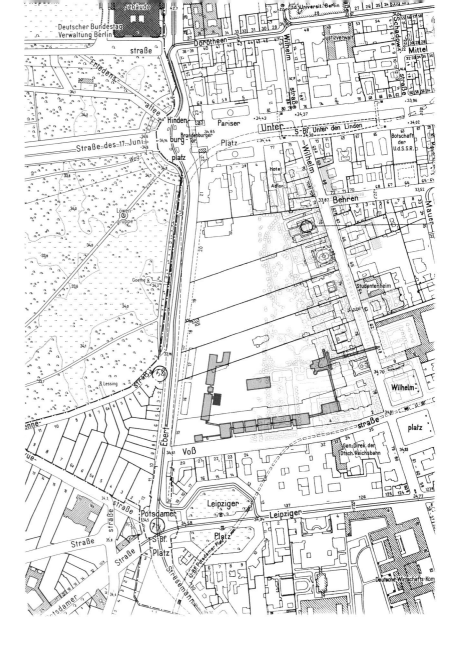

Detail of map with development boundaries before and after the last war, the Reichskanzlei bunker system (red) and the most recent development between Voßstrasse,

Wilhelmstrasse and the former Wall (blue).

Plan designs: Alfred Kernd'l
Technical execution: Verena Croon and Michael Eckerl

I would rather overlook many a political difference with Herr Caprivi than the ruthless destruction of ancient trees; he has abused the right to enjoy a state plot of land by damaging the same." Not even half a century after Bismarck's death this place was abused and destroyed on a scale that must have been beyond the imagination of even an Iron Chancellor, for whom even the loss of a few old trees in the Reichskanzlei garden was irreparable.

It is not possible to regenerate after total loss, but we can still draw on the authenticity of the place. It may hurt, but the bunkers are the only fixed points of the historic topography that can still be physically perceived here. For this reason alone they must be preserved in situ as accessible monuments. At the centre of power at the time, the frescos are evidence that is as accurate as it is authentic of the thinking of the Praetorians and their time.

On the basis of the bunkers and outline plans it is possible to convey a vivid description of the place and a historical view going back to the baroque period. Markings of old plot boundaries with the once famous house numbers in Wilhelmstrasse, special paving, that emphasizes the run of the excise wall and its more recent successor – all this must help to make things clearer. It is also necessary to secure archaeologically traces of cellars and foundations that may still exist, both to make it easier to fix former development boundaries and also for the possible integration into future development of any material remains that could make a statement.

Planners must further consider that in some segments at least it is possible to see how a typical garden used to be.

Bettina's nightingales, Bismarck's doings, Hitler's crimes and the post-war incision through the city must be able to impinge upon our historical imagination and our ability to reflect on the spot, not in a spirit of cheap mutual cancellation but as a juxtaposition of the heights and depths of our history. This intention could be supported if the highest executives of our state would reside in the area of the sites that were originally relevant. One prerequisite of this is historically aware town planning that does not immediately submit to any short-term requirement of commerce or private cars but is concerned to lay foundations of memory in its sphere of competence. They could also help to establish a kind of well-balanced patriotism in Germany at last, patriotism that survives without sackcloth and ashes and without yelling hurrah.

This is not helped by rushing to rename the most famous section of Wilhelmstrasse Toleranzstrasse. This banal and simultaneously involuntarily comic attempt to steal out of history is suitably complemented by the planned extension of Tiergartenstrasse through this area that is so steeped in history. Neither a zealous but misplaced desire to behave in an exemplary fashion in order to mollify suspicious foreigners, nor love of the car, should have the last word in this place.

THIES SCHRÖDER

POTSDAMER PLATZ'S BIG OPPORTUNITY? A SQUARE REFLECTED IN THE COMPETITIONS

New ideas for a place that has been passed on to us by written and photographed history as myth, as a lively urban area, as the busiest square and now the largest building site in Europe. But they are also ideas for the place that will continue to be concretely remembered as a piece of wild and romantic urban waste land, an empty place between the social systems of East and West, also manifested in their architecture. Between autumn 1989 and autumn 1995 six years of chequered fear and expectation passed: it was possible to talk to curious visitors when going for a walk across this urban steppe about winning this place back for the public, but also about self-representation by powerful investors. But all those visitors needed to make them enthuse about Potsdamer Platz was the lack of anything that had been there in the past or would be there in the future. In the meantime they are recognizably prepared to be interested in things that are recognizably new.

The years of a new approach to a place that was sold before thinking about how it might be used and the quality of that use have passed very quickly. But this senseless order of procedure and also developmental and architectural ideas, street spaces and urban public quality, high-rise buildings, eaves heights and block structures were discussed more aggressively in forums and newspapers than any other urban development problem had ever been.

A striking feature in the meantime, as the planning phase is largely concluded and building work is now a real feature in Potsdamer Platz, that expectations about new ideas for the square are not to become reality in this way. It is much more the "reacquisition of the European city" (Hilmer, Sattler), which came out of the urban development ideas competition, that is defining the target corridor for planning and building. Any chance of concentrating on really new definitions of an urban centre was removed from the agenda by this commitment. But the fact that this approach was also not implemented with the simplicity and clarity proposed by Hilmer & Sattler is a consequence of a further development stage in the planning discourse. This can best be described by borrowing a phrase from Daimler-Benz's former public relations director Matthias Kleinert: fear of slipping into a small-town mentality. In the course of the realization competitions held by the individual investors the "European" idea and dimension gradually shaded into stronger hints of the world-wide example of American cities. The only possibility that now remains for Hilmer & Sattler is designing the Potsdamer Platz railway station as an emblem of European urban development. When faced with the future image of Potsdamer Platz, critics who have experienced and been influenced by the United States feel increasingly reminded of the city centres in L.A., Houston, Texas or St. Louis, which is certainly not intended as a compliment.

The new Potsdamer Platz will not find its real form until the buildings are completed. Only when the area has started to be used will it become clear which of the many variations, the ideas that have been poured out about the myth of Potsdamer Platz because there was a chance of redefining it will actually become reality.

But how did there come to be so many ideas all at once about a place that had been rediscovered? The principal factor is that Potsdamer Platz stands at an intersection: it was formerly outside the city gates, then in the very centre, later destroyed, a warning to future generations, then forgotten as the two halves of the city turned away from it. And after 1989? Here East Berlin is joining up with West Berlin, this place is the first experiment in urban development – and as it is so much a focal point it is also used to observe and comment on the city as a whole. How is Berlin coming to terms with the reawakening economy, how are East and West coming to terms with each other, and how is Berlin, in the act of discovering itself, coming to terms with the international quality of a square? And above all: who does the city belong to? To the people who are building it, living in it, using it, paying for it? In Berlin's situation of rapid change, Potsdamer Platz was no more and no less than an example for the city. Now it is being built again. The planning and buildings tend to reflect the demands made on the city rather than the Berliners' and the place's idea of themselves.

But soon Potsdamer Platz will be an element that is taken for granted. By the turn of the millennium it is intended to be "functioning", as a place of international commerce and of elegant dwellings, of culture and of amusement. And so it will very quickly become clear whether the plans for Potsdamer Platz can deliver what they promise. For Potsdamer Platz as a place will remain at the centre of international attention as a part of Berlin's rediscovered self-perception. Potsdamer Platz will also be measured against its history: as a myth of a starting century and as a place of urban emptiness. Despite new buildings – these versions of Potsdamer Platz will be remembered. Whether they are remembered happily or longingly depends on the qualities of the new Potsdamer Platz, whose rebuilding was accepted by critics as a sign of development and had all sorts of visionary prophecies imposed upon it, ranging from "fiasco" to "hope for Berlin" (Manfred Sack in *Die Zeit*, 11. 9. 1992).

THE COMPETITIONS

A preliminary remark: the urban development and architectural competitions for Potsdamer Platz were not decided on the basis of their interpretation of the site. On the contrary, this square has become synonymous with an ensemble of places between the Kulturforum and Wilhelmstrasse, all of them near to Potsdamer – or Leipziger – Platz. All the designs are more or less neglectful of the square's history and significance. This means that in future Potsdamer Platz will be part of the cityscape much more as a place of investment than a lively square. This has led in particular to discussion about public places in the city.

This discussion began with the results of the urban development ideas competition, which was decided in August 1991. Discussion about the 1st prize for the concept submitted by Hilmer & Sattler's office in Munich has never ceased – right down to the decision of the architectural competition a year later. Hilmer & Sattler's urban development concept became convincing only in retrospect. The contribution was continually reproached with lacking elegant lightness, indeed that it was anaemic. Certainly the urban development idea for the area around Potsdamer Platz is not a critical reconstruction of Berlin's urban structure – neither in terms of eaves height nor of the traditional block structure. But the design is within the continuum of the European city. The simple building pattern, based on a system of clearly articulated blocks, admits mixed use and draws the eye to the public space, the streets.

The development competition was followed by a long phase of public discussion and discussion with the investors. The latter had commissioned Richard Rogers's office in London to draw up a master plan in parallel with the competition, and this was very positively received by many people. It led to a revision of the 1st prize, also in agreement with the investors' interests. The planning process was then set in motion on this basis, and at the end of it realization competitions were announced by debis/Daimler-Benz AG, Sony and A + T, a joint venture by Roland Ernst's enterprise group and the ABB concern. In August 1992 the Sony competition jury decided for the design by Helmut Jahn of Chicago, and in September Paris architect Renzo Piano's entry was chosen for the Daimler-Benz AG area. The A + T competition result was announced in 1994; Milan architect Giorgio Grassi's winning design places five individual buildings in a context that seems very peaceful.

The concept by Hilmer & Sattler's office is outstanding in its respect for the place, which is not reinvented, but above all reflects the historical layers in the Leipziger Platz area. Leipziger Platz will re-emerge as an octagon, with several streets meeting in the square in front of it, Potsdamer Platz.

Hilmer & Sattler foresaw housing provision from the very beginning; the city later agreed a proportion of 20 % residential area with the investors. But the transport concept remained unclear. Hilmer & Sattler had put in a plea for roads running exclusively above ground. And the structure of the green areas and areas of water remained in dispute as well. The first concrete decisions here came from a landscaping competition in autumn 1995.

After revision the design, which originally rejected high-rise buildings, admits differentiated height development with places emphasized in Potsdamer Platz and on the Landwehrkanal. But the basic structure of the design had been kept, and it was also not rejected in the realization competitions. Its real quality is this element of practicability. One crucial advantage: the urban development concept left the subsequent realization competitions the necessary scope for their own ideas. Nevertheless, one problem remains, despite retrospective esteem from several former critics: the concept was not strong enough to stand up to the various investors' interest in their "architectures". It had been so underemphasized and perhaps too much discussed, so that two of the architectural competitions with quite contrary results were able to claim that they had been decided in the spirit of the urban development requirements.

Urban development
ideas competition

1st prize
Heinz Hilmer and
Christoph Sattler,
Munich

Renzo Piano's competition entry does not start with the square itself, but at the point of transition to the Kulturforum. Piano's reflection of Scharoun's Staatsbibliothek is merely the clearest of signs of this.

Piano works on the basis of public space as the characteristic feature of the design area. The fresco-like presentation of his entry therefore shows spatial functional relationships between the buildings rather than anything else. The fact that he placed particular emphasis on the relationship with the Kulturforum ultimately secured the sympathy of all jury members. In fact the difficult problem of a link on the western side, which expressed its turned back in the form of the Kulturforum, and the Staatsbibliothek in particular, was scarcely considered in other entries – an unposed problem that did not reveal itself until a solution was suggested.

Piano does not develop the Kulturforum out of existence, but his design creates a transition to the block structure, no longer closed, that lies to the east of the competition area. Thus he remains faithful to the urban development requirement without taking it too seriously.

Another quality of the design lies in opening up the old Potsdamer Strasse as a pedestrian axis. And so that this does not bounce off the rear wall of the Staatsbibliothek, which is placed directly on the run of the street, Piano is planning a twin there, a Musical Theatre with a square in front of it, in other words an attractive goal.

The urban development structure of the actual competition area is of very high quality. The fact that high towers have been avoided to emphasize the Potsdamer Platz entrance situation put Piano's entry head

The 2nd prize in this competition went to Oswald Mathias Ungers, whose entry captivated people with its high urban development quality. The articulated complexes are defined above all by building typology.

Arata Isozaki's entry (3rd prize) provided for a collage-like mixture of building types. Here public streets and squares scarcely have a part to play contrary to urban development requirements. This design's metropolitan vision of office work brought it the commendation of "important contribution to the further development of urban architecture".

Richard Rogers's design won 4th prize. The concept as a whole particularly emphasizes the coherence of the district by developing raised edges to the blocks. But these building lines meant that the area was sealed off from the outside world.

Hans Kollhoff's design creates an independent quarter in terms of the Kulturforum and Berlin-Mitte. Kollhoff rejects symmetrical ground plans and creates an irregular network of streets that also makes the quarter lively in architectural terms. The jury picked out this design as a "manifesto against the urban development spirit of the time". It won 5th prize.

The special prize that had been announced went to Ulrike Lauber and Wolfram Wöhr because it provided an interesting alternative to the urban development requirements. The block structure prescribed in the general plan is broken up and brought together in large building complexes articulated in rows. The work was striking in its precise detail and "neutral elegance".

and shoulders above the rest. This omission is particularly good for Weinhaus Huth, which can be integrated into the structure of the district by this means.

Prizewinners other than the international Renzo Piano/Christoph Kohlbecker planning team with associated architect Bernard Plattner are involved in realizing the debis quarter in Potsdamer Platz: Richard Rogers, Hans Kollhoff, Arata Isozaki, José Rafael Moneo and Ulrike Lauber and Wolfram Wöhr are responsible for the architecture of individual buildings.

debis Immobilienmanagement, commissioned by Daimler-Benz to carry out the project, has pushed forward the concretization and co-ordination of the individual designs in discussion with the architects. The new debis headquarters, in the southern area of the central piazza, is placed as an urban accent on the Landwehrkanal. A 17-storey office and commercial building is set directly on Potsdamer Platz itself; south of this is Weinhaus Huth, which is a listed building. There will be areas of water north and south of the Piazza.

SONY Realization
Competition

1st prize
Helmut Jahn, Chicago

Sony's Realization Competition deviated from the Hilmer & Sattler plan by requiring that the public should be offered a large roofed inner area, the "Forum", rather than the street. Prizewinner Helmut Jahn's design created a definition of open space that was unusual for Berliners, and that was unable to avoid controversy in the city. While this approach is perceived by some as an "opening up of an internal space that is actually private" for the public, others fear a failure to relate truly open and public spaces to this central point of stages public space. A change of direction that was bound to cause discussion in terms of Potsdamer Platz's history as an open place.

The inevitable video screen, galleries, stages and niches for presentations of all kind – media presence is the key feature of Helmut Jahn's design.

Whether the Forum really is a modern continuation of the European, above all Italian, but also Berlin tradition of the arcade, as Sony insist, or commercial American design for self-representation by a concern, will probably not be decided until it starts to be used. At least this spacious complex will not founder on the unpopularity of the provincial approach to arcades, which are usually cramped and stuffy.

Jahn groups the other elements of his design around the Forum. The glazed roof of the Forum, the high-rise building and the Sony headquarters are particularly striking points. Light and more solid elements are placed alternately between these, intended to create interesting "inner-city" façades – a concession to the required building on the block periphery.

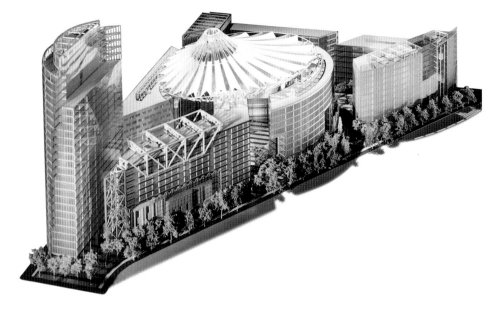

The design for the building complex – about 132,500 square metres of gross floor area – is by Chicago architects Murphy and Jahn. Sony and its partners Tishman Speyer and Kajima are the clients. At the heart of the office, amusement and residential centre is a 4,000 square metre arena: the Forum. Seven building units for various uses are grouped around this square. The Esplanade, for example, which is listed as an ancient monument, will be used for catering and events.

A + T Realization
Competition

1st prize
Giorgio Grassi, Milan

*ABB/Terreno-Roland Ernst's
A + T joint project is being
built on the south side of
Potsdamer Platz. The five
complexes have a gross floor
area of 74,000 square metres.*

Giorgio Grassi's design for the A + T project in the east of the Potsdamer Platz area reinterprets traditional building forms. Five blocks with differently expanded H- and L-shaped ground plans are placed in a row one behind the other; this design clearly deviates from the concept of closed street façades. A high-rise building on a droplet-shaped ground plan, on the former Haus Vaterland site, concludes this building complex.

The five buildings are solitaires only at first glance. The buildings are linked by a three-storey underground car-park and also by a ground floor arcade. Grassi's design radiates "urban dignity", the investors insist. This dignity is said to derive in particular from the reduced formal language of symmetry and a grid pattern.

Despite the involvement of three other architects (Peter P. Schweger, Jürgen Sawade, Roger Diener) in realizing the individual buildings the Grassi complex will certainly be one of the most reassuring sights in Potsdamer Platz. The area will need

this if it is otherwise to contain what has been announced. It could however be too relaxing, because of an excess of symmetry and above all the uniformity of the façades.

The Potsdamer Platz of the future needs identity. The fact that the relatively large number of protagonists and above all of "visions" made this claim increasing subject to disharmony will not necessarily damage the place and its quality in future. And yet the past of precisely this place, and the Potsdamer Platz myth, shows that contrasts only produce something special if they are in sequence. The transition from busiest square to derelict land and to the largest building site, for example, gives an idea of the tensions in between. But wanting to have a great deal that is parallel can make an artificial impression, like something staged. The Potsdamer Platz project is an experiment, and as such will remain permanently under observation.

OTHER PROJECTS (SELECTED)

Potsdamer Platz was formerly a transport junction. The development of the new centre and the architectural realization of the ensemble will make it a transport intersection again: an underground regional railway station will make connections with S- and U-Bahn (city railway and underground) and with regional trains possible on several levels. The underground regional station "Potsdamer Platz" is a key element in central Berlin transport planning.

The structure can be understood only in the broader context, as a new route model was devised for Berlin as part of the national transport plan. This is the so-called "mushroom concept". Fundamentally it consists of rebuilding and modernizing the Berlin inner ring, northern section, refurbishment of the Stadtbahn (city railway) and building a new north-south section through the city centre. The transport facilities in the central area are a key point.

The regional station, which will also give access to the new buildings, is 260 metres long and 50 metres wide, on three levels. After completion about 40,000 passengers will arrive, depart from or change here daily.

View from the walkway of Potsdamer Platz regional station and U-Bahn Line 3.

The underground S- and U-Bahn facilities are being reconstructed as part of the Berlin transport network rebuilding programme and the emergence of the new centre in Potsdamer Platz and the rebuilding of Leipziger Platz. A new U-Bahn line and Potsdamer Platz regional station will extend the network of routes.

The Potsdamer Platz S-Bahn station walkway will become an access level connecting the new railway lines as well. Two new stairways have been planned as the historic number of exits has to be retained and Leipziger Platz provided with direct access to the transport facilities. The first prize in the "Gatehouses in Leipziger Platz" competition was awarded to architect Oswald Mathias Ungers in October 1995. The design provides two pavilion buildings, reduced to their fundamental elements.

The symmetry of the buildings makes a gateway situation possible that addresses Schinkel's demolished gatehouses. The original gate situation was created by Karl Friedrich Schinkel in 1823/24. It created a spatial connection between Potsdamer Platz and Leipziger Platz. The resulting gate situation led to denser development in Leipziger Platz at the time.

Ungers's design makes it easier to find one's way in the surrounding urban space.

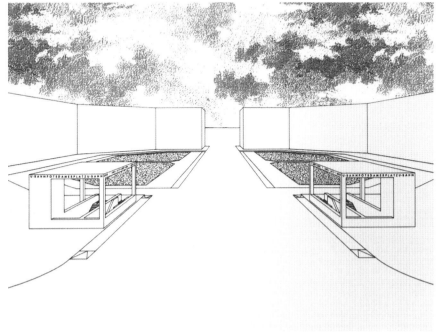

O. M. Ungers's design won first prize in the "Gatehouses in Leipziger Platz" competition.

The aerial photograph shows the area served by Baustellen-logistik Potsdamer Platz GmbH (baulog).

The much-quoted "largest building site in Europe" will be realized and completed in Berlin with the help of considerable input of capital by private and public investors by the year 2002. But the scale of the project and the site situation at the heart of a major city led to the decision to devise jointly organized supply and disposal for the necessary building materials. The resultant logistics concept has chosen rail and water, to benefit the environment and traffic flow in the city.

Baustellenlogistik Potsdamer Platz GmbH (baulog), set up in 1993, organizes this project, concentrating in particular on disposal of excavated soil, concrete supply, general cargo logistics, building site refuse disposal and ground water management.

Here are a few figures to make the demands clearer:

– Nine trains with 24 trucks and up to ten boats are used daily to remove about six million tons of excavated soil.
– Six trains carrying gravel or sand and two trains of cement travel daily for the production of an anticipated 1.7 million tons of concrete.
– Almost 100 meter-points take hourly measurements of the extent to which building site related ground water fluctuations have to be regulated; despite building methods devised to protect ground water it is calculated that 14 million cubic metres of ground water will have to be taken away.
– An average 1,000 tons of mixed cargo are transported per day, meaning two to three goods trains per day, to provide the building sites with building materials.

160

Energy for Berlin's new old centre is provided by Bewag – the Berliner Kraft- und Licht (Bewag)-Aktiengesellschaft, Berlin's power and light utility. An important requirement for supplying Potsdamer Platz – over a million square metres of offices, dwellings, theatres, restaurants, shopping arcades and underground car-parks – and other inner city areas is that a new combined plant (gas and steam turbine plant) is being built for the Mitte district power station between the Jannowitz and Michael bridges. This is Europe's most modern power station, and will function in a way that is particularly environment-friendly and energy-efficient; completion is planned for late 1996.

Bewag's Potsdamer/Leipziger Platz energy headquarters – in the picture: the façade at 120–122 Stresemannstrasse, near to the Prussian parliament – will cover power, heat and cooling requirements with the help of a transformer station and other plant.

After Hilmer & Sattler's architects' office was chosen to design Potsdamer and Leipziger Platz as a result of the urban development competition, Bewag commissioned these architects to design their premises.

161

Private bankers Delbrück &
Co.'s tower building is going
up at Potsdamer Platz; the
building was designed by
Sievers + Piatscheck + Partner
in Hamburg.

Revision of the 1992 design
reduced the tower to 17
storeys. This gives direct
access to a ten-storey base
building with a glass hall in
front of it on the Ebertstrasse
side. In contrast with the
tower section, which has a
glazed curtain façade with
supporting structures diagonally visible from the outside,
this building has a punctuated
façade. The principal visual
feature of the building is the
corner design of the tower.
The complex as a whole is
intended for retail and catering, office use and housing.

Photograph:
Gert von Bassewitz

162

*The Potsdamer Platz building site
from the south, October 1995.*

INDEX

Normal figures refer to the text, those in italics to the illustrations.